Rajen B. Harani has more than 21 years of experience in Banking and IT sectors. He has managed programs/functions across several business domains/geographies and has led many diverse teams. He is a Chartered Accountant (India) and a Certified Public Accountant (USA) by education. Rajen spends his off-work hours, mostly delving in writing. Till now, he has soft-launched various books on poetry, office-humour, cartoon and haiku. This is his first published book.

PAPER PALACE PUBLISHING
web: *paperpalace.in*

Names, characters, places and incidents are either the product of the author's imagination or are used fictitiously and any resemblance to any actual person, living or dead, events or locales is entirely coincidental.

ISBN: 978-81-940678-8-7

Thoughts and Experiences in Management

A collection of essays on various management topics

Rajen B. Harani

Dedicated to my dad, Bhagwan D. Harani

CONTENTS

I

INTRODUCTION

I like observing situations, settings and events. I also try to observe my behaviour in these situations and think about what I can do better. But of course, I always blame my human nature when I don't behave or utilize my skills as per my plan. Or when I can't learn or improve the settings.

Extending these observations to my professional life of over 21 years; I have witnessed various situations, studied scenarios and people and their behaviour in these situations. Slowly these observations became "experiences". On the other hand, the latest happenings around the world, the latest trends in leadership, management and professional world, books and articles written on various topics; helped me create some ideas and my own thinking "thoughts". Slowly I started writing about these "experiences" and "thoughts" on various topics; which has now resulted in this book "Thoughts and Experiences in Management".

This book contains essays on 30 management topics. So that way it is very easy to read. One doesn't have to follow any pattern to read. One can start from any essay of one's liking or of need and then jump to any other topic. You will also observe the tone of the books is forward-looking and positive i.e. what we can do to manage or improve the situation. This is predominantly because this was written as my guide book in management. Now that all 30 odd topics are bound in one book; I am hoping that I can improve and enhance my managerial skill. Hope the reader of this book also finds these useful and practical. These essays have been written over 2+ years so you may see some variations in my writing as clarity or experiences improved, but then the management is about continuous improvements!

Wherever necessary (and you may comment more than necessary☺) I have used famous quotes to enhance the reading or lighten up the heavy stuff. I have sourced these quotes from the internet.

I have got immense satisfaction in writing this book. The whole process was very rewarding. Starting with a situation or element of management (mostly from the recent experiences e.g. hiring essay came to me when I was doing a lot of hiring for my department), then to get my experiences into a structured text, mix with that my latest thinking or few words about how to improve the situations and then finally get the essay out on paper – this whole process was quite exciting. Of course, writing on management is bit tougher than say writing poetry or cartoons (I delve in both these so this is first-hand experience). In poetry or fiction, one draws power from emotions. In Management this is not easily possible (at least that's what I think of). And maybe that's why both these genres are considered quite different i.e. fiction and non-fiction. But writing with my own experiences may have helped me to write with rigour by drawing some emotions from my experiences.

Finally, this is my first attempt at getting a book published. Thanking you for buying this book and encouraging budding writers like me.

– Rajen B. Harani | ra_bh_h | Nov 2019

2

MOTIVATING OURSELVES

Motivation is an industry in itself. Nowadays one will find that many courses are being offered on this topic as well as find numerous books on this topic. This essay covers my current thinking as to how to motivate ourselves in our daily professional life.

"I think it all comes down to motivation. If you really want to do something, you will work hard for it." - Edmund Hillary

Larger perspective and goal

With our day to day tasks, meetings and achievement focus, we all sometimes forget to connect with the larger perspective of our life and its ultimate goal. Every person's trip in life is different and based on that everyone should have a larger goal (not just monetary or positional but one that connects with your inner core). It can be anything that you feel strongly about e.g. increasing your creativity, connecting with humanity or your spiritual journey etc. Typically, these goals are very difficult to identify and quantify - the very act of quantifying these bring them down to materialistic level. However, I would suggest everyone should attempt to define larger perspective/goals in their life.

"Only I can change my life. No one can do it for me." - Carol Burnett

List Maker

We should make lists of our "to-dos". Tasks required to be completed for home, for office, for social stuff and the family. Listing tasks gives us a ready roadmap of things to complete. We can then rank these tasks onto Important and Urgent scale. Trying to prioritize the important stuff and completing them regularly. Slowly and steadily we all would get into the habit of knowing what is pending, what is done and what is important. We will start feeling great about ourselves and will not have that nagging feeling that something is missing or missing to be done. We would have either completed that important task or would have the situation under control with the list at our command.

Clarity of thought

Once the larger perspective and day to day task list is with us - we will start getting clarity in our thoughts. We would not unnecessarily try to chase something that is "what we don't want" and will not have bad feelings about those. We will value our time and utilize it wisely.

Drop the news

We all know that more than 80% of news (that's what I feel) that are sold (and generate TRPs) is typically negative. Again most of this news is about things that we don't use for our day to day life. Surely then reading this news is not going to motivate us. If we can't avoid then at least we can de-prioritize news from our lives. A real tough one - but worth trying?

TV again?

I have nothing against TV/Movies or entertainment. We all know that while watching the shows we train our minds to avoid creativity i.e. avoid doing creative work ourselves. We get into a passive mode and of course waste time. More time on TV/movies means more time away from our larger goals/perspective.

Pat on the back (whose? yours!)

Who is the best person that can motivate us? Surely, it's us. So keep on patting your back once in a while. Smallest of victories - let's celebrate and motivate ourselves.

Give without expectations - help without reciprocity.

We all have experienced that doing something for us gives us pleasure. However, have we also experienced that doing something for somebody else gives us more pleasure? No? Try it! It's true.

Let's try to give without expectations and help without expecting reciprocity.

Bad company?

We can get motivated with bright and cheerful people and at the same time get demotivated with people who are always complaining or cribbing. Surely it's very logical to avoid their company.

Connect with the unconnected

Connecting with your family (hey! that cousin from overseas), friends (your school buddies) or neighbour from another city will take you back to your roots and help you remember your non-fuss days. These old relationships were quite pristine without any hierarchy and once you connect you may still find them at the same level.

Books? Oh yeah!

Definitely. Read books and on a variety of topics. Real knowledge and information about the world and life's perspective comes from the books. You will know that you are not the only one that is suffering or going through that phase of life. You will find inspiration from some character or real-life story to regain your energy and move on!

Hobby Hobby - are you there?

A hobby is a great tool for de-stressing. A hobby helps us to be in a positively present zone and unites us with our core. Having a hobby is a great way to motivate ourselves. After a long day in office; learning music or planting trees in your garden is a refreshing thing to do!

My Mentor - where are you?

Mentor is the one who challenges you, gives correct advice and shows the mirror. He/she is also helping you to be realistic with goals in line with your strengths and weaknesses. Having a mentor is a great motivating factor in our lives. Try to get one!

"We talk on principal, but act on motivation." - Walter Savage Landor

Mirror Mirror on the wall

Mirror reflects our physical body; likewise, the mind is a great reflection tool to reflect our thoughts, beliefs and ideas. Reflecting upon your day, idea or action is required so that we do course correction and achieve our goals. Thinking is the best way to spend time. Reflecting is a good and much-needed tool for motivation.

Health is Wealth

Nothing gets achieved without the body. Worth remembering this and taking good care of our body with the right exercise and proper nutrition. No fun in achieving a lot of materialistic stuff by compromising our health.

Meditation, anyone?

I have not tried this one yet - but heard a lot of benefits of this. Worth trying?

"Finish" that meal!

Finally, more we finish more we achieve. This leads to fulfilled dreams, leading to happiness and increased motivation. It's a positive spiral - try being the finisher!

"People often say that motivation doesn't last. Well, neither does bathing - that's why we recommend it daily." - Zig Ziglar

3

STUFF THAT WE MANAGERS DON'T DO ENOUGH

Deep down we know that we as managers don't do something well or enough. We all can improve and also know that constant improvement is the key. The things that I have presented are the common themes that I have seen amongst various managers - of course first being me!

"Success in management requires learning as fast as the world is changing." – Warren Bennis

Understanding Customer Problems

How many times we genuinely discuss customers' problems? Customer can be an internal customer (other department/group) or an external (to whom we sell our services or goods). However, we don't spend enough time to discuss, debate, analyse and understand customer's real issues. We all have a ready (already cooked and historically agreed) notion about what customer needs and easily accept this hypothesis. I am not saying that all customers are also aware of what their real issue is? [Wow I am now pushing the boundaries too much and challenging my customers also?] However, I feel as professionals we need to assist our customers in discovering (and then serving) the real problems.

I feel I need to improve my understanding of customers operations, processes, challenges and problems more often and more in-depth.

Delegation

We managers all believe and in principle agree that we should empower our staff, give them authority & responsibility, let them experiment and fail and make them independent. But do we do this? Do we genuinely empower them? And let them also know that they are empowered beforehand and not just when things fail we let them know they were empowered throughout!

What we end up doing is assigning tasks. This is not delegation - delegation comes with full empowerment and full authority of the given assignment.

[This is also covered as an essay topic under a separate chapter on delegation]

Taking time out for planning future on your own (not just when it is demanded from you)

We generally plan when we are asked to. Deadlines for budget, for the next project, for completing the review of business or submitting plans for future.... we thrive by the dates already pre-decided for these activities or when pushed onto us. All we end up doing is meeting the deadlines and doing a poor job of planning.

We as owners of our functions should be planning at every step, every decision and building our Book of Plan that can be used when formal plans are demanded. Planning is also a creative process - the looming deadlines can't help create a Mona Lisa.

Improving processes on the go (and as part of regular practice)

Do we challenge the embedded and well-established processes? Do we genuinely worry about improving things? Do we wish to engage in genuine process excellence exercises? Do we improve processes/operations so that our staff can focus on more value-adding activities? Do we all do this as a regular practice?

The answer is well known.

1on1s with team

Formal meeting about a project with members of staff is not 1on1. Believe me, I have seen managers telling me that they already have many meetings daily with their staff. They feel these would suffice as 1on1s. I also end up losing count of 1on1 meetings that may have been compromised.

"Good management consists in showing average people how to do the work of superior people." - John D. Rockefeller

Asking "Why" (about what we do and how we do stuff)

The TED talk by Simon Sinek will explain this. You will find this easily on the internet.

Do we genuinely know why we do - what and how we do the stuff?

Stop worrying about the *Circle of Concern* and start focusing on the *Circle of Influence*

Operating in the Circle of Concern will end up making you a whining person. Only way to succeed is to focus on the Circle of Influence. You will find a lot of material on this topic on the internet.

Not always end up doing what is urgent

Classic - Eisenhower's Urgent/Important Principle - Using Time Effectively, Not Just Efficiently.

We all know about this, have read about and have noted about this but we all end up doing what is urgent.

"Practice Golden-Rule 1 of Management in everything you do. Manage others the way you would like to be managed." - Brian Tracy

4

TREATING YOUR JOB AS A BUSINESS – BENEFITS AND HOW TO GO ABOUT IT

"My son is now an 'entrepreneur.' That's what you're called when you don't have a job." – Ted Turner

In today's fast-changing world the business models are turned upside down overnight. Businesses themselves are sold like commodities and everywhere business services are aggregated. New technology is killing old business and garages are turning into disruption laboratories. In this amazing new world; business and businesspersons are constantly evolving themselves to survive. New methods of service deliveries are created. However, at the same time, customer loyalty is becoming fragile. In this revolution of everything-is-changing-you-better-be-changing-else-you-are-gone-tomorrow; one thing which is not changing and not evolving is the way "we the employees" treat our employment and go on doing things like what we have always done.

"Uber, the world's largest taxi company, owns no vehicles. Facebook, the world's most popular media owner, creates no content. Alibaba, the most valuable retailer, has no inventory. And Airbnb, the world's largest accommodation provider, owns no real estate. Something interesting is happening." – from internet source

The employment or job that we are doing is still being done the same way as it was done in the 90's. We still treat employment as a barter exchange where we the employees are selling our "skill and time" in exchange for "regular weekly or monthly payments". We treat employment as a fair deal where we give away our time and efforts (sometimes with motivation and dedication and sometimes without) for money. Each of us based on the availability of opportunity and results that we achieve will get promoted to the next level (eventually!).

"Even if you are on the right track, you'll get run over if you just sit there." – Will Rogers

I believe we are not far away from revolution affecting the employment, the way we get employed and the reasons the businesses need employees.

My suggestion in this evolution is to treat our employment as if we are running an enterprise called "me". Treating our job as a business is not a bad idea – however, it sounds "crazy".

In this way we would constantly be connected with ever-changing world, we would be agile; we would be treating our services as sales and fairly treating our customers "the business and its departments". When the world moves into interconnected micro-entrepreneurs (I believe this is already happening) running their own business without the need of employment we would still be around and thriving.

Let's explore this (crazy) idea a little further and see what steps we can take to build on this idea.

"You are not your resume, you are your work." – Seth Godin

All businesses typically have 3 main things to worry about; (1) Sales (2) Production and (3) Finance. I have also read in some book that to succeed you need to take care of these 3 aspects. The book had gone further and had recommended that as a business person you need to make sure that your top 3 executives are leading these 3 activities. Best people running sales, production and finance is all you need.

In the case of a business called "me", the best person to lead all these activities is definitely "me".

Production: Your services or output that you generate as part of your job is what you produce. That is your production. Try to map out your output and define KPIs of what you term as success. Discuss with your boss and department heads what production output goals that they would need from you. You can also find this out from your appraisal goals if your company has some system for performance tracking. Make sure qualitative aspects of your job is well understood and what is "good' is generally understood by you and your boss etc. Once these benchmarks are established relentlessly focus on your output (i.e. Production) and treat this with utmost priority. Mentally always remind you that "your business" needs "you" to produce "your best".

Sales: Your production is just one part of your job. You need to constantly engage yourself in selling your wares. Be aware of your reputation (brand image) and status (brand recall) with all people that matters (typically your boss, department heads and other senior people). Don't be ashamed to "sell" your business i.e. you. Market your achievements, demonstrate your production and constantly remind people about how good your product is! You may need to give out free samples (work done free for other departments, helping out others without any return benefit), engage in marketing (find new opportunities and markets for your employment), build brand recall (be visible in social events, participate in extracurricular activities). Remember sales are critical for any business to succeed. Your competitors (other employees) will always be around. You will need to watch out their activities as well and always come on top.

Finance: Remember your salary is cost for the company. Always see how you can justify your cost by increasing your production and improving the quality. In your activities try to find out ways of saving overhead costs and also opportunities for turning the cost centre into a profit centre. Along with your sales acumen and your production, your financial prowess will see that your business (i.e. you) is always successful.

"To be successful, you have to have your heart in your business, and your business in your heart." – Sr. Thomas Watson

The main philosophy that you need to imbibe is not treating everything for granted i.e. I have done my job now I deserve to be paid well and the company should treat me fairly. In the "business" that you run the fair game doesn't apply as the survival of the "smartest" is the key. The key is with you all you need to do is implement it and start running the business called "you".

"Business is a combination of War and Sport". – Andre Maurois

5

WHAT REALLY MOTIVATES PEOPLE TO PERFORM THEIR BEST IN A TEAM?

"It benefits us all to motivate others." – Karrueche Tran

I have always wondered what motivates a team to perform at its best; why some teams perform well and why some don't.

The easiest answer that we get ourselves convinced with (rather easily and that too knowingly) is "Money Motivates People". I also challenged myself whether this is correct. However, when reflecting upon the career journey I found this answer is not correct. Based on what I have seen and experienced so far; Money works but only the halfway; the real motivation in a team comes from various other (and thankfully quite manageable) items. I am sharing my thoughts with all those who can read this. Of course, this essay is reflecting my current thinking on this topic. Like all things in life, things change including items affecting motivation.

"Motivation is the art of getting people to do what you want them to do because they want to do it." – Dwight D Eisenhower

Sense of Purpose

This is the real thing. People like to contribute to the cause which provides them with a Sense of Purpose that is worth enough to fight for. The Purpose that challenges them to overcome their differences and that satisfies their inner feeling of connectedness with the world at large. The Purpose of a team, its project, its challenge is the key defining item that motivates members of a team. However, just having a Great Purpose is not enough; it has been communicated to the whole team and communicated constantly with dedication. And who does this communication? Leader...!

"An employee's motivation is a direct result of the sum of interactions with his or her manager." – Bob Nelson

Leadership and its participation

2nd most important item for motivation is the team's Leader. Just having a named Leader is not enough. The Leader has to be actively participating. The Leader which communicates with the team of its Purpose, which reminds the team of its duty, supports the team in challenges and directs it in the crisis. People die for people who are ready to die for them. The Leadership that provides this trait will see the Team succeeds in most of its endeavours. However, just having a Sense of Purpose and Leader is not enough. Team's Goals have to be clearly defined and articulated.

Clearly Defined Goals

Defined Goals / Articulated and well-understood Targets and Action plan that support Goals achievements are necessary for a team to succeed. Like that proverb "If you don't know where you are going, any road will get you there", a team without goals will be a well-oiled army without any enemy or grounds to concur. A team really requires defined Goals that they achieve and celebrate on its way to its Purpose. Goals help the team to know that they are on correct the path. Leadership is the best which defines the Goals and celebrates each achievement with team members.

Freedom (to do things and especially, to fail)

High performing teams don't like a controlled environment. What it requires is "Freedom". Freedoms to take decision, Freedom to have their small battles, Freedom to innovate, improvise and do creative things on their way. Freedom to, not to just do things but also fail while doing things. The team which owns up its failure is most effective in achieving larger goals. Along with freedom, most team members would die for one more trait i.e. Respect.

Respect (can be loosely also be read as Recognition)

One more thing that Motivates members of a team is "Respect". This mostly refers to the Respect they expect from their Leader. However other teams, organization and its various departments also provide this Respect. Respect is a simple trait which can be easily delivered by the organization and its Leaders but generally ignored. People mostly focus on "Rewards". In my opinion, it is the Respect that people are hungry for and not just "Rewards". Respect provides more Recognition (for the members who are receiving it) than the "Rewards". Rewards are reactive whereas Respect is a proactive step.

Development and Growth Opportunity

A high performing team is well aware of its achievements. The members are constantly checking their progress and reflecting upon their journey. They know their real worth. The team which sees greater clarity in individual members' Development and opportunity for Growth will keep on contributing at the best. This is also the main reason the team members will start leaving the team. Once they feel that the "Purpose" is achieved the bonding becomes lose and the individual growth targets will take over. However, if members are aware of the growth path then they will stay put and will try to achieve their own Goals while still performing at its best.

"Motivation is everything. You can do the work of two people, but you can't be two people. Instead, you have to inspire the next guy down the line and get him to inspire his people." – Lee Iacocca

6

WHAT IS YOUR INFORMATIONAL EMPOWERMENT QUOTIENT?

It would be cliché to say that in this "Information Era" [this word is also a cliché :-)] Information is power. We all know that correct and timely actionable information is of essence and is one of the key differentiators between the winners and the losers. The world is becoming more and more complex and although a huge amount of information is easily available, the right information with the right people at the right time is still a problem area. Competition of natural/ man-made resources is thing of a past and wars are now won or lost based on information. New emerging knowledge economy where information aggregation methodologies drive the business model; the "Information" remains the most precious and at the same time underutilized (or rather under circulated) commodity.

Information is a powerful tool and can easily be transferred, reciprocated and increased. It's not an exchange commodity where both parties have to let go of it in exchange of what they receive. Rather it's a multiplier commodity where both parties' post exchange account is double of the original before reciprocation.

Information is not only a powerful tool for new economy businesses and for corporate wars; but also a good tool for an organization's internal processes and functions. It is that lubricant which allows the organisation to function frictionless. It is a powerful empowerment tool and letting the right people possess the right amount of information at the right time is the most logical thing to do. But alas; what I have seen that information is often hoarded.

I believe in sharing information and creating internal transparency. In my view approx. 85% of the information that we receive or create is easily transferable without any impact on the organization or the person who is sharing the information. Yes, for that 15 % of cases; the information sharing can be avoided or used on a need to know basis.

Haven't you seen those cases of large programs failing to meet the deadlines or completely miss the "real" requirements by not sharing information with the right people at the right time? Didn't you notice that the correct people were not identified? The information was not shared with respective Subject Matter Experts (SMEs) at the right time and the status reports /requirements are not widely circulated to a larger audience to seek feedback?

Sharing information is empowering the people; whether it is empowering subordinates or seniors. Timely, correct and actionable information is always useful at the hand of the recipient.

In this essay, I would like to argue why information sharing is good for you and what are the advantages and what pitfalls you avoid.

"I believe in decentralized management that includes a lot of delegation, empowerment, and accountability." - Anthony Scaramucci

Big Picture Advantage

How easily we can miss the big picture if we are always engrossed in nut and bolts without knowing what the purpose of our action is? How this purpose is made available to staff and vendors? By sharing the Big Picture.

Haven't we heard Lewis Carroll's famous quote: "If you don't know where you are going, any road will get you there." If you don't share the big picture via information sharing believe me your staff is already taking any available road.

Make sure that you communicate the companies/department's (a) Purpose (b) Goals and (c) behavioural attributes that you propagate with all concerned by regularly and repetitively communicating and sharing.

This sharing will help people to align with the Big Picture.

Avoid "Not My Job" disadvantage

Sharing information will make your people understand the common goals and challenges. They would see how their peers in the same circle or other departments are doing and would understand the overall responsibility circle. They would understand how their actions and activities fit into the larger functions.

All this will yield to better understanding of shared responsibility and the feeling of "Not My Job" will be alleviated.

Sharing information about other departments, other companies, peer groups to your staff and superiors is always a good idea.

Increased Loyalty

Sharing information with staff, seniors and the peer will empower them. This will also increase their loyalty towards you and they would feel connected with you. Information can be of any nature; very basic such as your leave plans to advanced information such as your company's strategic directions; all information will empower people surrounding you and they would be loyal towards you.

Feedback loop: Avoid heading towards the wrong path

Information with the right people; especially with SME of processes/functions is the most desired. These are the people with the required know-how to comment and provide feedback. If the information is kept with a chosen few then diversity of thought and feedback loop is restricted.

If you are not getting the right feedback about your programs, progress, process and products then you will not be able to keep abreast with the latest advancements and will miss out on an opportunity or worse head towards the totally wrong direction.

Increased Camaraderie

Sharing information and that too in a common platform makes people feel equal and equally empowered. This will increase the camaraderie amongst the recipients of the information as they are seeing that nothing is kept hidden and everybody receives the same amount of information. Slowly they would also start contributing and sharing information and common sense of purpose will prevail.

This ultimately will yield better results.

Increased Sense of worth

People receiving information will feel that they are appreciated. They would feel that they are part of the circle and they are looked upon as contributing to the organization. This will automatically lead to better connected and motivated people will again lead to higher productivity.

Easily identify New Opportunities / New Ideas

In a true "free flow information" environment new ideas and new opportunities will be easily identified. People will not hesitate sharing information and their ideas. People will share ideas, brainstorm, carry out new business/ideas proposal and share with

Proactive Threat management

Likewise, the connected employees will not be fearful to share any bad news or threats. They would be open to share their assessments of the future with seniors and future threats will be easily managed.

Known and Clear Accountability

Once information is easily available and flowing, people will find it difficult to hide behind organisation charts or processes. Clear accountability will be visible and on the face of people. This will automatically identify and sort out people with bad performance and meritocracy will find it easy to germinate and take root.

"If you want to publish data, you should do it to share knowledge."
– Andrew Ng

7

SUBJECT MATTER EXPERTS AND THE VALUE THEY BRING

"Wise people understand the need to consult experts; only fools are confident they know everything." - Ken Poirot

We all have worked with Subject Matter Experts (SMEs) also known as (a.k.a) functional people or domain experts. The chances are that the reader of this essay is also an SME or has an interest in becoming an expert or manages one or is working for one. This essay is written in the context of software development but subject matter experts are found in all walks of life or all departments in an organization.

I have dealt with SMEs throughout my career. In some aspects, I too am an SME of my field of SDLC and Project Management. In this essay, I will share the values (apart from the subject matter expertise) the SMEs bring about, what these groups of people tend to do and how to keep them engaged. These thoughts are purely based on what I have experienced and seen and some elements of generalization are embedded in these thoughts.

"The top experts in the world are ardent students. The day you stop learning, you're definitely not an expert." - Brendon Burchard

The values (over and above the subject matter expertise) the SMEs bring about:

Create a boundary-less organization - SMEs tend to ignore the organizational boundaries or departmental/silo mentality and focus on the problem at hand. SMEs across departments (and in some cases across organizations) connect quite well without any pangs about the hierarchy or politics of the organization. This way they create a parallel boundary-less and knowledge-driven organization in its own right.

Industry connect - The SMEs typically are connected with the latest happening in the industry and follow the latest developments in the larger context. This is a good trait to continue being an SME. However, organizations tend to be less nimble in connecting with larger changes outside. SMEs mix well with other SMEs from different organizations and easily share the progress/latest happenings.

Truth - The SMEs don't hesitate to call a spade a spade. If the situation is bad they directly call out the problem and have already moved onto thinking about the solutions. They are least interested in playing the blame game and focus on the truth. This way they are also conscience keeper of the organization if the organization utilizes them well.

Focus on output - The politics and related matters do not interest the SMEs. They are keen to use their expertise and have focus on the output /results. They are not paper-pusher or bureaucrats but skilled technicians who have love for the output and like to see the results of their efforts.

Knowledge retention - SMEs have keen interest in knowledge retention within the organization. I have seen numerous instances of SMEs being called upon even after they have left the organization. They don't have any hesitation of passing of the knowledge and voluntarily train their backup.

Big Picture - Being output-oriented SMEs can easily focus on the big picture and contribute towards various problems. They typically have an organization's interest at heart and can easily connect the dots.

So you would say if SMEs are so great at what they do then why don't they run all organizations and tend to be the backroom players?

Good question - let's see what are the reasons that make SMEs typically the backroom players.

The classified ad said, "Wanted: CEO needs a one armed consultant, with a social sciences degree and five years of experience."

The man who won the job asked, "I understand most of the qualifications you required, but why 'one armed'?"

The CEO answered, "I have had many consultants, and I am tired of hearing with each advice the phrase 'on the other hand'."

Typical Tendencies of SMEs:

Dislike Politics and all other related aspects - The SMEs genuinely dislike politics. They can't stand it nor engage in this. They are poor in understanding undercurrents and are the fall guys in most cases. They also don't appreciate the organization hierarchy that well and tend to bypass the rule of command. These traits don't help their cause in latching onto big jobs.

Hang onto the old - SMEs being the SMEs that they are; generally, are purists and love the old style of the world. They have cynical views of everything shiny and new. Most likely this view gets created as every time a new world is promised to them - they have seen that their methods have saved the world once the new methods have failed.

Philosophical - Many a times SMEs become too philosophical or dreamy about the truth and right behaviour; that they lose out by going against the current. They don't easily jump into new bandwagon which is typically sponsored by seniors in the organizations.

Less pragmatic - SMEs being purists tend to miss out the whole pragmatic aspect of 80/20 principle. 80% correct to them is compromise in the organization which struggles to meet the costs vs. output challenges.

How many consultants does it take to change a light bulb?
We don't know. They never get past the feasibility study.

SMEs even though don't tend to become the rulers of the game; are heavy contributors and heavy hitters. If not properly engaged they tend to lose interest or worst leave the organization. We want our experts to be the experts and continue to help the organization to continue making strides towards perfection.

"What's an expert? I read somewhere, that the more a man knows, the more he knows, he doesn't know. So I suppose one definition of an expert would be someone who doesn't admit out loud that he knows enough about a subject to know he doesn't really know how much." - Malcolm Forbes

How to keep the SMEs engaged (and retain them):

Functional challenge - As far as possible keep the SMEs engaged in some mental pursuits/challenges. The more problems you through at them the happier they are.

Platform for internal departmental discussions/industry discussions - Make SMEs your ambassadors of knowledge internally and externally. This way they are fully connected and continue to gain knowledge for them to continue to be the experts for you.

Managerial support - Remember SMEs are not at best traversing the organization landscape and definitely require help in sorting out "how to go about in this scenario" like situations. Be ready to jump in and help them out.

Empowerment - One thing you can be relaxed that SMEs will not tend to misuse the empowerment that they are provided with. They will remain true to their promises and at the same time like to take on more responsibilities.

Respect - this is the least difficult thing that you can do for the SME group.

8

ROADMAP FOR CAREER MANAGEMENT

In this essay, I am putting forward a few ideas that will help us in managing a fulfilling career. However, these are not my thoughts alone but the result of a brainstorming session I conducted with my teams and some experiences and readings added on top of this.

I am going to present three broad themes that will help us build our career and strengthen our will for our professional pursuit.

Principles

These are basic principles - the very tenet of growth and advancement in our lives. Be it professional corporate job or your own business; these principles and their adherence becomes the foundation of any career.

Whose ownership?

"If you don't do it, it won't get done. And if you don't do it now, you probably won't do it at all." - Patrick Pinckney

You are the owner of your career. If you don't plan, implement or worry about your career! Who will? One has to take the reins of the career in his/her own hands and don't wait for others or fate to make it happen!

Who is responsible?

"They always say that time changes things, but you actually have to change them yourself." - Andy Warhol

Responsibility of taking action about all aspects of one's career is with the self. One can't be responsible for circumstances, chances, luck or background; but one has to be responsible to act!

"All business depends upon men fulfilling their responsibilities." - Mahatma Gandhi

Blaming others or cribbing won't help you

In this journey of career management; blaming others or cribbing about your situation will not help. It may reduce your stress for that brief moment but it won't make things happen for you. Blaming is the easiest and natural escapist trait that we all have been through but it won't help you.

"All blame is a waste of time. No matter how much fault you find with another, and regardless of how much you blame him, it will not change you. The only thing blame does is to keep the focus off you when you are looking for external reasons to explain your unhappiness or frustration. You may succeed in making another feel guilty about something by blaming him, but you won't succeed in changing whatever it is about you that is making you unhappy." - Wayne Dyer

Self-reflection

Regular self-reflection is a good tool to use while we build plans for our career. Having your capability and commitment under check is always the right thing to do. Unless we self-reflect we won't be learning from our failures and improving ourselves.

"A man must find time for himself. Time is what we spend our lives with. If we are not careful we find others spending it for us. . . . It is

necessary now and then for a man to go away by himself and experience loneliness; to sit on a rock in the forest and to ask of himself, 'Who am I, and where have I been, and where am I going?' . . . If one is not careful, one allows diversions to take up one's time—the stuff of life." — Carl Sandburg

No free lunch

Nothing comes free. Everything requires efforts and your career growth won't be a free lunch. If you need to build your career you will have to pay for it with your efforts, commitment, hard work and risk-taking.

"There's no such thing as a free lunch." - Milton Friedman

Required attributes

Having seen the principles on which we can build our career; let's now see those critical attributes that would take us there. These are quite self-explanatory; however, I will use a famous quote to ring home the message.

Having passion

"Passion is energy. Feel the power that comes from focusing on what excites you." - Oprah Winfrey

Having fun

"Fun is one of the most important - and underrated - ingredients in any successful venture. If you're not having fun, then it's probably time to call it quits and try something else." - Richard Branson

Perseverance and consistency

"Nothing in this world can take the place of persistence. Talent will not: nothing is more common than unsuccessful men with talent. Genius will not; unrewarded genius is almost a proverb. Education will not: the world is full of educated derelicts. Persistence and determination alone are omnipotent." - Calvin Coolidge

"Success isn't always about greatness. It's about consistency. Consistent hard work leads to success. Greatness will come." - Dwayne Johnson

Staying focused

"Successful people maintain a positive focus in life no matter what is going on around them. They stay focused on their past successes rather than their past failures, and on the next action steps they need to take to get them closer to the fulfilment of their goals rather than all the other distractions that life presents to them." - Jack Canfield

Self-confidence

"Self-confidence is the first requisite to great undertakings." - Samuel Johnson

Hard work

"Luck is great, but most of life is hard work.: - Iain Duncan Smith

Concrete Steps

Having understood the principles and attributes; now let's move to a few actions or steps that we can take to achieve that dream of a great career.

Set goals

"Setting goals is the first step in turning the invisible into the visible." - Tony Robbins

Plan for long term and short term goals. Study your situation, bring out your dreams on paper and then list down your goals. Goals will help you navigate your long career journey and explain where you are heading.

Once they are written, regularly review them and keep them handy. This will help you to stay focused on the path. Goals will remind you what you are up to and will inspire you for that long, arduous journey called "life".

Perform SWOT

SWOT analysis is a tool to map out your strengths, weaknesses, opportunity and threats. This analysis will help you focus on your strengths, minimize your weaknesses, and take advantage of opportunities available to you while avoiding the threats that you face in your career.

Have a mentor

A mentor is a guide and adviser who will help you in your career journey. Typically a mentor is a person who is not directly related to our organization hierarchy nor has any direct influence in our career. First and foremost quality of a good mentor is one who has our interests in the heart.

Having a mentor will help you to carry out introspection, study the circumstances and be prepared for adversity. Mentor will also keep our emotion and negative energy in check.

"What you want in a mentor is someone who truly cares for you and who will look after your interests and not just their own. When you do

come across the right person to mentor you, start by showing them that the time they spend with you is worthwhile." - Vivek Wadhwa

Upgrade and up-skill

For achieving your goals and in line with your weaknesses and threats you will need to upgrade and up-skill your selves.

"Roads do not upgrade or maintain themselves. Bridges do not repair themselves or rebuild themselves." - Martin O'Malley

Perform!

Finally, once all things are done what remains is the "action".

"Do you want to know who you are? Don't ask. Act! Action will delineate and define you." - Thomas Jefferson

9

DELIVERING INTANGIBLE VALUE

"Strive not to be a success, but rather to be of value" - Albert Einstein

We all know that to be successful in any business one has to deliver value to the end customers (and of course to other stakeholders that get involved in the whole chain).

For small or start-up businesses; value delivery is the only thing that will distinguish that business from already established large businesses. Customers will only get involved when they see value in engaging with that business. In a large, established organization; even though the value chain is well established, they still have to constantly be on their guards to remind the whole internal supply-chain process about delivering value to the end customers. Customers' loyalty can't be taken for granted and once a customer gets the wind of diminishing value they will sooner or later leave that enterprise for another one that offers value or better value.

However, this value is just not measured in the money term i.e. am I getting goods or services worth the money that I have paid? But it is the whole experience of securing goods or services. If this is not the case than businesses which are charging higher for their goods/services would close down. Because this is not just money's worth calculation it involves some intangibles as well.

"Business is all about the customer: what the customer wants and what they get. Generally, every customer wants a product or service that

solves their problem, worth their money, and is delivered with amazing customer service." - Fabrizio Moreira

Here I will try to describe some intangibles that I could think of.

Satisfaction with the whole process: This involves everything from the process interaction with various counterparts to the timely service. The whole gamut of dealing with the supplier's organization can be bucketed into this. E.g. you may have seen that once you get a poor service you generally don't prefer to that establishment again. It may be a shop next to your house or service station where you get your car serviced.

Respect: Respect can be covered as part of customer satisfaction as well – however, I want to point out this as a separate value. Customers even though may not want to be treated like kings (though we always tell that the customer is king) - they would, however, like to be treated with respect.

Empowerment: Customer should feel empowered to make choices. If there are numerous products available (say TVs) they would not like to be told what to buy and what is good for them. If they feel that a decision is being forced upon them they will leave. Customer should feel (and not just feel - it should be the reality as well) that the final decision is theirs.

Feeling of a fair deal: If customers don't get a feeling that they got a fair deal vis-a-vis the cost they incurred - they will leave the suppliers' organization with a bad taste. Each customer should feel and be treated fairly. This involves transparency, shortcomings in the product, other choices that are available and relative features.

Association with customer / Same as me: Customer may also derive value if they feel associated with the supplier. It may be a friendship or alumni association. They may derive value in being associated with supplier "same as me".

Contribution: Customer may get value if they feel they are contributing to a cause which they feel associated with. It may be a social cause or say contribution towards the country's development. If a supplier can establish that connect - customer may derive value from it.

Communication and Advice: During the longer duration of a service e.g. painting contract of the house - constant communication as well as seeking suggestion from customer may get them involved as well deliver intangible value.

"The customer is the most important visitor on our premises. He is not dependent on us. We are dependent on him."- Gandhiji

An organization which plans for delivering one or more of such intangible values will be successful. Smaller organization with their owner-controlled delivery - this is possible and must for growth. For a large organization, it should be a constant internal check that will keep on reminding the system for delivering value to the customer.

"The best customer service is if the customer doesn't need to call you, doesn't need to talk to you. It just works." - Jeff Bezos

10

IMPROVING EFFECTIVENESS (A BRAINSTORMED ESSAY)

I had carried out a brainstorming session listing down "things" that we can do or start doing that would make us more effective. The session was intended to list down only "few" things in 20 minutes. However, 15 of us could list 30 such "things". Each of us then decided to choose 5 things that each of us will strive to improve in the coming years. The stress point of the brainstorming session was to list things that would make us "effective" and not necessarily "successful" as we can only change/improve things that are in "our" control.

"Without continual growth and progress, such words as improvement, achievement, and success have no meaning." – Benjamin Franklin

Following is the list. Not in any order of importance - I have retained the exact verbiage that we used in the session.

- Being patient (or being more patient) with a situation or people
- More Greet and Meet (a.k.a improve networking)
- Result oriented discussions (conclusion /action seeking)
- Improving focused approach towards our tasks/actions
- Towards matured behaviour (or improving our maturity)
- Being more appreciative of others
- Informal connect with stakeholders/customers
- Knowledge sharing
- Improving team bonding
- Punctuality in meetings/calls/tasks/promises

- Proactive approach
- Principled behaviour
- Challenging ourselves
- Taking ownership of things/situations rather than blaming
- Prioritization / To-Do lists
- Keeping purpose/objective in mind
- Know your B/C/S (Boss/Colleague/Customers/Suppliers)
- Email etiquette/better-written communication
- Improving our presence/attire etc.
- Improving presentation skills
- Managing our brand image
- Setting out expectations before committing on anything
- Situational awareness
- Accepting and acting on "situational" leadership
- Holiday planning/handover
- Seeking regular feedback from peers/seniors
- Being self-aware
- Continuous learning - functional/technical aspects
- Market awareness
- Big picture

II

ON INNOVATION

The official and the most apt definition of the innovation goes like:

Innovation is production or adoption, assimilation, and exploitation of a value-added novelty in economic and social spheres; renewal and enlargement of products, services, and markets; development of new methods of production; and the establishment of new management systems. It is both a process and an outcome.

The best part of this definition is the last sentence. Innovation is both the process and the outcome. Guess this is well summarized by M S Dhoni as follows:

"I have always believed that the process is more important than results."
- M S Dhoni

If the process of innovation is well established then the outcomes will not be surprising. In today's world where innovation (read innovation with tools such as ML/AI/Cloud/Apps) is the most talked-about subject; the innovation is being considered as something that is externally fitted and has to be specifically invoked. However, I believe in innovation that is continuous, part of the culture and embedded within the organization.

Now I will touch upon this topic in detail.

"Culture eats strategy for breakfast" - Peter Drucker

Let's consider **what is innovation or rather what innovation results in**. This is a better yardstick to measure the innovation efforts.

Here I will use some terminology from earlier established philosophies such as TQM, Kaizen and others. I am not talking about the size of innovation but the concept of innovation.

Production of Better Products or Better Production of the Products: Yes, both are considered as innovation. Either new or better products or new or better methods to produce products - ultimately better / cheaper or enhanced value services to end customer is considered as innovation.

Improvement from yesterday: Even small - if there is some (and conscious) improvement in either the process or in the end product - that is innovation.

Enhanced customer delivery (with or without extra costs): If customer experience is improved (and of course recognized by customer) then it is innovation.

Use of fewer resources: If the same thing post innovation consumes less of the resources (money, power, time etc.) then it is innovation.

Capacity release: If nothing has improved but some additional work capacity has been created - that is also innovation.

Make things less risky (or what they say make the world a better place): If the efforts have produced an environment that is less risky than earlier - then it is surely innovation.

"You have to have a big vision and take very small steps to get there. You have to be humble as you execute but visionary and gigantic in

terms of your aspiration. In the Internet industry, it's not about grand innovation, it's about a lot of little innovations: every day, every week, every month, making something a little bit better." - Jason Calacanis

Now that we have seen what innovation is or what are the results; let's now see what can be done to improve the quantum of innovation in an organization.

Involvement and Attention (especially of senior leadership): to drive innovation culture; the senior leaders have to be involved and pay attention to the efforts being made. The whole journey of innovation is a long one and can't be treated like some event.

"The simple act of paying attention can take you a long way." - Keanu Reeves

Celebrate small wins: Innovation doesn't always have to wait for another great product to come out - small wins (which collectively go long way) should be identified and celebrated.

Encourage tinkering and failure: Encourage members to experiment and fail once in a while. After all, Thomas Edison didn't fail in thousands of attempts to create the light bulb, just identified thousands of ways as to how not to create a bulb.

Have events but encourage everyday creativity and innovations: Many times we have seen large events being held to encourage innovation. Nothing wrong with this but this should not be just restricted to that 1 day out of 365 days. Everyday culture of innovation should be encouraged.

"Once you have an innovation culture, even those who are not scientists or engineers - poets, actors, journalists - they, as communities, embrace the meaning of what it is to be scientifically literate. They embrace the

concept of an innovation culture. They vote in ways that promote it. They don't fight science and they don't fight technology." - Neil Tyson

Empower and encourage usage of new technology: Empower members to experiment with new technology as well as cross-collaborate with other departments/streams to foster sharing of ideas.

"Collaboration and augmentation are the foundational principles of innovation." - Vaclav Smil

I hope with these steps a culture of innovation takes root in an organization which in the long run makes it an innovative one.

"The culture is what creates the foundation for all future innovation. If you break the culture, you break the machine that creates your products." - Brian Chesky

12

TIMING - THE INTUITIVE ARTISTRY

Timing is the moment when something should be done or something should happen.

In the financial markets, advice given to all investors is to "never time the market". However, this may very well work in markets, where the virtue of wait-n-let-it-grow-with-passiveness-of-long-term-focus is applicable but I would not advise this for any other streams of life - especially in job or business that you are in.

I believe timing or doing things at an exact moment is one of those artistry things that is very difficult to master. However, with practice maybe we can move towards this mastery.

You may have seen that politicians are very good at this. If something has gone wrong in a country then the opposition party is very quick to pounce upon that situation and may make a hue-n-cry about it. If something has gone right (even at times without any support from the ruling party) then the ruling party will go to market (i.e. electorate) immediately with the good news.

Though we don't have to become politicians to become master in this - but we should take a cue from them and try to work on our timings. If you have come so far - then you would say - I get it but can the writer expand a bit - can he come to what's-in-for-me?

"You don't have to swing hard to hit a home run. If you got the timing, it'll go." - Yogi Berra

To understand this better I will give two examples from our lives.

Say there is some new regulation going to hit your industry - members in your company are equally perplexed and anxious about the future. Your boss has informed about this in a team meeting but you can see he doesn't know much and is equally anxious to know. You also know that eventually, the situation will become clear and some modifications in process or products will be required. You also know that typically new regulations will bring the consultants into your organization to explain these things. Now how you will take this situation? Remember your promotion is due! A few days passed - the regulation is now out but it's all legal mambo-jumbo. I guess you are getting where I am going - if you want to come out as a star in this situation and target that promotion - this is the most opportune moment. Get your networks working for you and try to seek help from your friend who is a legal expert to come up with a basic draft of what is the impact and present to your boss. At times of uncertainty, even the smallest amount of right information will help in the long run. The boss will take this to his boss and so on. In the end, you would have timed the matter perfectly. The effort that you would have taken will not be much as it's still basic draft - but you got your boss talking to his boss and made him a star for the day - this will make a huge impact on your promotion chances.

You are in a project meeting - some tasks are getting allocated. You can see that the project is hugely important but is delayed. You are going to get some task. You have a choice to select any task. Which one you will select? My advice - select two - one easy and other relatively tough. Why? the 1st task - you will complete in no time and will remain in the green zone and for a second you will have some time to work out an arrangement. If you help the situation or make the project to go in the green zone you will come out as a winner.

Now I will go into a few **general principles or ideas which will help us to improve our timing in a professional setting.**

Under promise - over deliver (but in time or before time)

Always promise less than what you can do (if possible ask for more time than required) - but deliver always before time and more than what you have promised.

Feel the air - pounce on new thing or uncertainty

Volunteer to explore new things. The downside is very limited but the upside is huge. Understand that anything new or seemingly challenging then even your seniors or bosses are uncertain - so your timing to choose these tasks will not go unnoticed.

Regularly report status

If the regular status is demanded then send in advance and if no status is demanded then provide voluntarily to everyone. People are always happy to receive some unsolicited status report - that makes them in the know of the thing and make them feel important.

Network to know what is coming or what's happening

Timing is always related to some information. If you get hold of information then it will be easy to execute on timing - network and know what's come and what's happening in an organization

"You win battles by knowing the enemy's timing, and using a timing which the enemy does not expect." - Miyamoto Musashi

Hope you agree with me. The timing is an intuitive art and I am still at the basics of this art.

13

SOME THOUGHTS ON KNOWLEDGE MANAGEMENT

"In the long history of humankind (and animal kind too) those who learned to collaborate and improvise most effectively have prevailed." - Charles Darwin

Knowledge Management is that one stream of management where everybody agrees with the need for it but at the same time, everybody struggles to implement it. Most knowledge management initiatives start with good intention but down the line, the effects/utilization remains challenging. Thus this essay. Caution: I am not at all expert in this field of knowledge management but will try to summarize my current thinking on this topic.

"The only thing to do with good advice is to pass it on. It is never of any use to oneself." - Oscar Wilde

So before we start on how's of knowledge management - let's re-cap what is knowledge for an organization?

Again I will take liberties in this essay - so please bear with me.

In my opinion, knowledge is anything that is:

- reusable information geared towards improving organization efficiency or value delivery
- information about repeatable steps that can be utilized for training or in actual processing of similar artefact

- collection of common understanding of facts/truth/ capability within an organization
- information about who has the necessary information in case that is needed
- proprietary product or process level information which is crucial for the organization's delivery
- collection of issues faced and solutions that were adopted
- learning from the past mistakes or feedback loop (e.g. customers' feedback)

Of course, this is not the complete list - but you can get the gist - reusable, repeatable, learning, facts/truth - everything that can be utilized for organization's delivery (and/or with improved efficiency or values).

"Knowledge is like money: to be of value it must circulate, and in circulating it can increase in quantity and, hopefully, in value." - Louis L'Amour

Now that we have understood the concept of knowledge; let's see what should be done with knowledge or in other words what are the **objectives of knowledge management** system?

Geared towards improving efficiency of the processes or better product creation

Knowledge management process should help in improving efficiency (faster / better) of the processes and/or produce better products - I guess this is the ultimate objective - without this what is the purpose of knowledge management?

Empower and Assist members of the organization to save time and focus on value addition

Knowledge management should help members to save time so that they can focus on higher value-adding activities.

Improved customer service

Knowledge's purpose it to do better things; which includes improved/better/enriched customer service

"We are drowning in information but starved for knowledge." - John Naisbitt

Now let's see what needs to be done with the knowledge management process or how to go about building the knowledge management system.

Build small: instead of building a monolithic knowledge management system - try building a small system or systems. Instead of the tree - start with a leaf. Make this successful and use the lessons elsewhere

20/80: plan for taking care of that 20% of the knowledge which generally caters to 80% of the scenarios

Incentivize usage or maintenance: I have seen this to be the major problem. The system is in place but nobody maintains or uses the same

Make it part daily habit: make it part of the DNA e.g. like checking emails.

Top / down seriousness: we have seen many a times tools are left to very junior part of the organization - nothing wrong with it - but seniors should not totally ignore the same. They should contribute as well as discuss the metrics around the same openly

Build simple to use tools: if the tools are not easy or accessible then usage will suffer

"Knowledge management will never work until corporations realize it's not about how you capture knowledge but how you create and leverage it." - Étienne Wenger

14

SOME DECISION-MAKING HACKS

"Thinking is the hardest work there is, which is the reason why so few engage in it." - Henry Ford

Imagine it's a Sunday morning and you are sipping a cup of coffee. You are sitting on your laptop and doing the most important activity which is requiring your full attention. Your spouse and kids are nearby going on with their normal routines. Your important task is going to impact all of you as it's about your next "family vacation!"

You are going through various locations, comparing various hotels, flight paths and rates. Amazing amount of material and options are available on the internet. You have simultaneously opened 12 websites and your thumb and finger in unison press the alt+tab at your command. You have a fair idea but choosing between thousands of options is hitting your nerve.

After 45 minutes you are now seeing a pattern and you emerge half-victorious and announce to your family that you have made a decision on location+hotels+flights. Your spouse approaches half-assured and peeks into your choice of location and hotel and mumbles something about the location. You argue back saying it's a beautiful place and your office colleague has already gone there. You have now passed the hurdle number 1 (at least it seems) - spouse moves on to the hotels and picture gallery. And there goes the voice you were afraid to hear "See the room photos! Are we going to stay here?" and continuous "why you are always choosing the bargain hotels, at least sometimes take us to a decent hotel!" and walks off. You are doomed - the lunch seems now long away and you are back to the grind. You go back to your "research" work. This whole process is draining your energy! This decision making and choosing is a tough job. Tougher than gardening work, tougher than running 10 miles and tougher than spending 2 hours with your brother-in-law where he constantly talks about his achievements!

Decision making is a tough activity. It saps energy, makes us weak and constantly scares us away from the whole process. You are also afraid that you will make a wrong decision and suffer disproportionately! Not sure when human started making decisions but maybe our brain is still wired just like that caveman "homo sapiens" who for thousands of years didn't have to make many decisions. Maybe apart from running after hearing any sound!

"In my house, I'm the boss, my wife is just the decision maker" - Woody Allen

Over the years through experiences, learning from reading books/magazines, doing my research, observing others doing it and learning the hard way by failing; I have created my list on decision making for various scenarios. I am sharing these decision making hacks with you.

Busy Bee

Suppose you enter some organisation's office where you want to get some things done. Suppose you are a supplier of theirs and want some paper/certificate from them. You estimate that the work will take 2 hours but may require you to come 2/3 times more. You enter into a hall where 7 to 8 members of staff are occupying their seats. Like a small kid entering the school premises for the first time, you observe all of these staff members. The 1st is busy doing the work but is alone, 2nd is likewise busy and surrounded by few people just like you, 3rd seat is vacant and looks like not occupied since morning and 4th is free and seems to chat with other people who are also loafing around....so on so forth and you make a mental note on all of them. You see that some are free, some are relatively free, some are relatively busy and some are super busy!

You have to make a choice and decide on whom to approach. Once you approach a person there is no going back.

What to do?

My decision hack?

Go with the busy bee - the person who is the busiest! "What?" you will go wild in your mind "why can't I go to the person who is free and having time?".

The Law of Inertia states that a body in motion will remain in motion, and a body at rest will remain at rest.

Remember the person is busy because he/she is doing work and choosing to do the work - the person who is free (and assuming that there is work available to do) is free because he/she is choosing to remain free. There are more chances of getting your work done with a busy person as your work is just another task - she/he is already doing 9 tasks and adding one more task, adds just 10% of the work. However, for the free person, your task is the addition of 100% of the work. Just think about the inertia working on him or her!

Super Employee - In the Flow

This is similar to the above - however in your own office space. Suppose you are managing a fairly large team of 20 people. All of them are having similar experience and you know their skills quite well (which are mostly similar). You know their relative workload and already have a mental note of their "busy-ness". You know that some of them have bandwidth available to pick up new tasks and your most valuable (highly rated) employee, unfortunately, is super busy but happy doing and you know that she is the flow.

There comes your boss - he wants something urgent - required in the next 2 hours. The task will require you to stop doing your current activities and focus on this urgent task. However, you will require additional help.

Whom should you call? Your "yes-I-have-bandwidth" employee or "i-am-super-busy-but-in-the-flow" employee?

My decision hack?

Go with the super employee in the flow. She would accommodate other work, understand the priority and with inertia positively flowing would easily help you complete the task.

Remember super employee has reached this space by repeated doing the work.

"We are what we repeatedly do. Excellence, then, is not an act, but a habit" - Aristotle

What gets written gets done

Your memory is super sharp, you go from meeting to meeting and are known as a person who completes the stuff! You get things done and fast. You are going on a vacation for 10 days and before that have attended various meetings. You have called your staff individually and given them instructions on the half-done tasks and tasks that need to be completed before you come. Your work that is pending - you have taken mental note of those. Some meetings that you attended with senior folks - you were the scribe and are supposed to send minutes of meeting. For this one meeting, you have taken notes.

10 days' vacation.

You are back.

What gets done?

My decision / Choice hack?

What was written; by you for your tasks, by your staff for their tasks.

"The things that get committed to paper are the things that are committed to in life. And the things that get scheduled are the things that get done" - Robin Sharma

Once you are back; you will see your notes for that one meeting where you had taken - you will send minutes. Your staff that were noting things down have most likely completed their tasks. Those who were just nodding their heads have not done their tasks - you wonder what was it but then both sides have forgotten!

Crowd fewer stores - depends what you want

Suppose you want to buy some FMCG items for your home. You see a big supermart where thousands of people are enjoying (?)

their Sunday afternoon. Some are following their kids and wife, some are standing in long queues and some are just playing with trolleys by taking them from one place to another. You hesitate before you enter the store. Before entering you notice a small mom-n-pop store next to this supermart selling the items that you want. Surprising the staff is all looking at your invitingly! They don't seem to have many customers. You think....where to go?

Now suppose you want to buy some local delicacies. There is this big store which is quite famous for the stuff that you want to buy. Scenario is the same. Some are following their kids and wife, some are standing in long queues to get the stuff and some are struggling to pay the money to the counter as it is already full of people who also want to pay money. You hesitate before you enter the store. Before entering you notice a small mom-n-pop store next to this superstore selling the same stuff that you want. Surprising the staff is all looking at your invitingly! They don't seem to have many customers. You think....where to go?

My decision hack?

For standardized FMCG stuff, the free store is good for you and for the specialized stuff you better go where you have to fight to come out victorious.

No fun standing in queue and wasting time for buying toothpaste and no fun in not standing in queue and saving time to buy a bad tasting delicacy.

Money grows on trees - literally!

A few years back few of my acquaintances were behind me to buy investment products in some teak wood plantations. The offers were quite luring. Money doubles in a few years and all those great things. Some of my friends invested in these securities. I did not.

Similarly a few years later new schemes came asking people to invest in some agricultural land parcels which will then converted into development lots of non-agricultural lands when the growth of that area happens. Some of my friends invested in these land parcels. I did not.

My decision making hack?

Nicely summarized by Mart Twain."

"I am more concerned about the return of my money than the return on my money." - Mark Twain.

Needless to say, my friends lost their hard-earned money.

The prestigious client who complaints a lot and other is a silent one

Imagine you have two clients. The 1st is this prestigious client that has given you a consistent business for many years. You give special service ensuring that repeat business is guaranteed (and is always). This client is lax in payment but you deem that is the norm with these great and big orders giving customers. This customer gets special services from your staff as everybody knows the special status. Smallest of the complaints and your staff travels to their factories deep interior in the country. Most people talk about this customer in your office and quote the big orders that keep coming. There are some products returned (for no reason did you say? no the product was not suitable for their need) but that is part of the business. Your company is very happy with this customer.

Then there is this customer who is not that big. Who orders the exact product from your catalogue and understands your speciality. Payment terms? Of course, what you demand! Complaints? Not many - seems happy. Manages the problems on its own. Some repeat business but that is decent not like that prestigious client.

You come up with a free service scheme and a very good discount scheme to encourage more sales. You are confident that by offering this scheme to both customers you will generate new business. Whom you will offer that 1st?

You know your answer.

My decision hack?

Go for the silent one.

Reason? Profitability rate! No loss due to returned products, your payment terms, and no cost incurred to serve this customer! And frivolous complaints!

"Customer who pays you the least complaints the most" - Anonymous

Incentive to fleece you

You want to get your car repaired. Car is making some noise lately; surely it is that belt and maybe the air conditioning system. Maybe something else. Big? Don't know - you are not the expert. You have to rely on expertise here! But some big expenditure is expected.

You know this mechanic who opens on Sunday (hey the time suits you) and you have generally heard about him. He is quite free and can easily take your car for repairs. You have also heard that there is this other mechanic who seems to be busy but is fast. He has a lot of business and no time. He is so tired by Sunday that he strictly observes Sunday holiday. You may have to go late to the office on Monday after dropping your car with him.

My decision hack?

Go with the Sunday holiday guy. Why? He is quite busy and has a lot of business - for him, your car is just another car where he has to devote his time and generate the revenue. The incentive is to complete your car as soon as possible so that he can focus on other cars which are in the queue. He is not worried about generating sales (not open on Sunday) and knows that money is in the flow. There is no incentive for him to give your wrong treatment to generate more revenue.

The Sunday open guys is free - has less business. For him your car is a special kind - he would find faults that you may not have heard. After all, he is the specialist. There is an incentive built in to overcharge or give specialized and costly service that you may not require!

This hack would work in all specialized services; medicine, career guidance and admissions to courses, repair work at your home, etc.

(This hack is based on an article that I had read in The Economist. I have experimented and found to be true)

15

SOME THOUGHTS ON STRESS-FREE TIME MANAGEMENT

The topic Time Management is very simple to understand and is intuitive/ingrained in our psyche. However, with every passing day, we all feel that the days just pass by and we remain unfulfilled and/or under-achieved. We then start taking stress of this under-achievement and waste more time.

Here I am presenting some thoughts/ideas/suggestions on improving or streamlining our time management skills.

Any road will take you there

"If you don't know where you're going, any road will take you there" - Cheshire cat to Alice in Alice in Wonderland

Time available with everyone is limited and if we don't have a concrete idea as to what we want to achieve then its waste of time from the word go. The best and oldest suggestion to write your tasks/goals still works. Writing down (or creating list in tab/laptop/mobile) your "things to do" is still the most important time management advice.

Once you have written the stuff - you can review them regularly, change the priorities and feel satisfied when you see things getting completed. The satisfaction of striking a task completed reduces stress and motivates you to achieve more.

Urgent and Important

"What is important is seldom urgent and what is urgent is seldom important." - Dwight D. Eisenhower

Everybody knows the Urgent / Important "Eisenhower Matrix" but the key question is how many of us practice it?

Using the 1st principle to write your tasks and then marking the tasks into these 4 categories will immensely help you. You will notice that your important tasks are getting the right amount of focus and you start feeling less stress.

Monkey and the Tennis player

Imagine that each undone task is a monkey on your shoulder. Surely you will feel the burden of "the monkey zoo" when you will review your task list. This monkey zoo becomes more burdensome when you are waiting for somebody else to feed the monkeys i.e. or contribute in completion of your task. The angry monkeys will scare the life out of you or scare you to take the full-on stress ride.

When you are waiting for some inputs or contributions from others then it's time to brush up your back-hand tennis shot. In these situations try to keep the ball in others' court. Hit hard and let other people know (and others as well who are witnesses to your tennis match e.g. your boss, colleagues or friends know) that the ball is in their court. Let the monkey be on their shoulder. This will clear your task list and reduce your stress. Monkey once fed will return happily to you and may walk by your side holding your hands rather than on your shoulder.

Juggling works in circus

You are attending a teleconference, catching up on your email, offline speaking with your colleague and checking your mobile for urgent message and most importantly all these simultaneously. You are born juggler. But then a few hours later you come back to recollect what was achieved and like most times you can't remember what was discussed in the teleconference call and which was that message that you wanted to reply.

Multitasking even though seems fun and cool; is highly overrated and cause of unnecessary stress. It's better to concentrate on one thing and do that with full attention rather than being a juggler.

Spinning is fun! Are you sure?

We all are quite busy and do a lot of stuff during the day. We go to meetings, attend conferences, create documents, review and respond to emails... You get the drift. We like action. We talk highly of the person who is full of zest, energy and actions and like to emulate him or her.

However, before we hit the road of action it's better to check whether that road is going anywhere or it's just the roundabout that seems like the road. In other words; a lot of actions maybe just spinning at the same place without achieving much. Actions do not mean achievements. Actions with direction and purpose will lead us to achievements. The direction and purpose comes from sitting in one place and thinking. Unnecessary actions take away important time from us which we could have spent wisely on sitting in one place and think.

Weekends come at the end of the week

Most of us try to keep a lot of our household chores exclusively for weekends. During the week we try to focus on the official/professional tasks. The home-stuff comes only at the weekends. However, by Friday evening your energy is drained and you don't get your exclusive tasks completed during the weekends as well. Rather than keeping all household tasks for the weekend you should start chunking these tasks and try completing them during the work weekdays. Household chores will also give variety to your workweek and days will not become monotonous.

16

THE FOLLOW UP (AND NOT JUST IN SALES)

"Our greatest weakness lies in giving up. The most certain way to succeed is always to try just one more time." - Thomas Edison

You may have seen the classical diagram (see below) about sales-related effectiveness of follow up; I feel that a similar technique is required for all walks of life; especially in management.

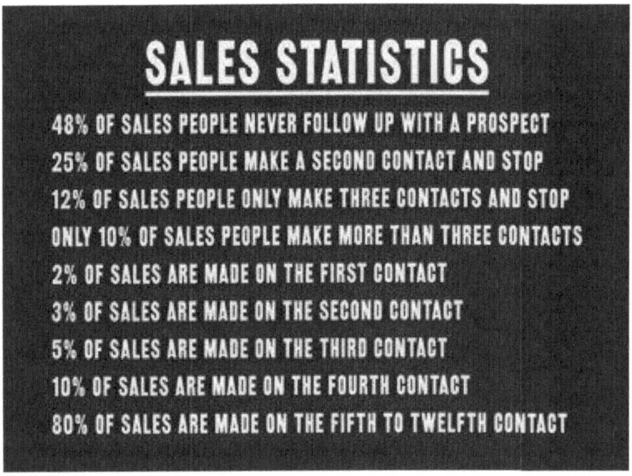

So let's understand what is follow up?

Classical and appropriate (for our context) business definition goes like this "something that is done to finish a previous action or make it more successful."

"Either you follow-up or you fold-up" - Bernard Kelvin Clive

I guess the importance of follow up is generally well understood. The question is why do we stop ourselves (and talking about me!) from following up?

Here are the reasons that came to my mind:

Inhibition: guess we feel that following up will not look good and we stop to act freely

Why bother? (or it will not yield result) : we try once or twice but give up or we think that grapes are sour

Lethargy: we just are bound by inertia, science does its job :-)

Will spoil relationship: we feel that too much (how much is too much?) follow up will spoil relationship

no system: we don't have an appropriate system for following up - we just go haphazard and then give up

lack of motivation: we just can't motivate ourselves for doing one more follow up - we still remember the result of last follow up :-)

we get busy (aha! the classical reason): we just get busy in other stuff and forget

You may say, Rajen, "Yes follow up in sales is understood, but where in general management the follow up is required or needed?".

Follow up is needed everywhere - just a few examples in office context:

- approval on proposal

- selling ideas
- waiting for budgets
- getting claims/invoices/purchase orders released
- checking whether your tickets are booked
- reaching to contacts within or outside your organization for any work
- or even in finding lost emails

....you get the drift!

So what's the solution? What would help us to improve our strike rates of follow up?

I don't have a perfect solution else I wouldn't be writing this; but here is a list that I prepared for myself.

- use different channels: email, personal connect, phone, letters - be novel
- demonstrate what's in for me: don't just follow up from your viewpoint - show the WIFM as well
- respond to other people's follow up: remember - everybody is in the same boat
- keep connect: not just when in need
- build system: write down, standardize the processes
- give away free value: sometimes just provide free and unsolicited value
- follow up after work is done: complete the loop
- Guess this list is enough. If I can implement even half of this - I believe I will be fine.

"Motivation is what gets you started. Habit is what keeps you going." – *Jim Rohn*

17

DOING THINGS RIGHT AND DOING RIGHT THINGS

"Do the right thing. It will gratify some people and astonish the rest." - Mark Twain

We all have seen situations - most likely in your office or factory or wherever you are working. Things are being done, not just that these things are being done but things are demanded to be done "Rightly". There are rules and regulations and status checks and reports which show and demand that things are done rightfully and correctly. These things are seemingly important for everybody and from top to bottom in the organization, everybody is required to perform these things sincerely, rightfully and obediently. I have experienced such situations not just once but many times throughout my career.

I am not suggesting that all this is wrong; only suggesting that many a times such situation where people are doing things right there has to be constant scrutiny as to whether Right things are being done or not!

I will give you an example from many years ago. In one such group where SLDC testing was being performed; there used to be levels of reporting towards upward chain of hierarchy about progress of testing life-cycle. These reports starting with junior most test analyst would get reported to the next level with details being replaced with "high level" information so that the next level could understand in "their language." After the fourth level, the information was made so "easy to understand" that any information what so ever usable for progressing on the things at hand i.e. "Testing" was completely lost. This fourth level report used to be so generic that one can use in any organization, any project and for any year!

People were made responsible for publishing these reports on time and strict penalties were applied if one missed any of the deadlines for these reports. Over time the underlying testing as an activity; used to be forgotten for weeks together and "reporting" was taken as "primary" activity for everybody involved. Classic situation where "Thing done Right" but nobody worried about "Right Things Done"!

Surely nobody plans for this situation to arise but this is a result of inefficiency getting built overtime.

Following are the reasons (per my understanding) as to why these situations are found.

- Organization's mission/goals not necessarily communicated or well understood
- Empowerment maybe give a mere lip service
- Incentive models incentivizing wrong things
- Questioning senior management not encouraged
- Ego worshipping encouraged
- Middle managers afraid to take bold steps
- Independent decision making not encouraged
- Bureaucracy has taken roots quite strongly
- Delegation not found/ not encouraged

Following are my simple suggestions to make the situation where "Doing Right Things" is encouraged instead of following the mantra of only "Doing Things Right".

- Communicate, Communicate, Communicate - senior/middle managers to focus on spreading the company's/group's goals/objectives/mission to all levels in the organization/group
- Get senior/middle managers exposed to "clients" more often
- Challenge each process/paperwork requirement ruthlessly
- Encourage questioning/start grievance process/ suggestion box process
- Train managers on delegation
- Review Organization Structure / Group Structure for ensuring easy connection of junior-most members to senior-most
- Encourage Open Town halls
- Encourage transfer of members between functions for spreading freshness
- Incentivize correct behaviour

Hopefully, you would agree with me. Please don't take me wrong - "Doing Things Right" (i.e. Execution) is as much important as "Doing Right Things" (i.e. Goals/Mission/Why and what we do) - however forgetting "Doing Right Things" and only focusing "Doing Things Right" - would lead to destruction.

"With a lot of things in life, it's hard to do the right thing." - Cat Zingano

18

EVERYDAY CREATIVITY @WORKPLACE WHY, WHAT AND HOW OF IT

This essay is quite close to my heart for various reasons. Obviously not because that I am a creative person (far from it :-) or that I am an artist (neither), but because I firmly believe that everything that we do brings about our creativity, our chance to stand out, our part of that larger contribution - even though in very small or minuscule way.

When we generally think about creativity we think about creators such as Michelangelo, Picasso, Einstein or Kalidasa from the fields of Art, Dance, Music or Science. We can't imagine creativity in our day-to-day life or creativity at our doorstep that can be executed or undertaken by us. We always think about that large picture - we don't think that creativity is simply put "connecting the dots with various things and producing something unique".

"Creativity is just connecting things. When you ask creative people how they did something, they feel a little guilty because they didn't really do it, they just saw something. It seemed obvious to them after a while. That's because they were able to connect experiences they've had and synthesize new things." - Steve Jobs

Creativity can be demonstrated in various ways; obvious creative outputs such as producing new musical notes, or new product or new ways to solve a scientific problem or painting etc. However, I believe that the report we produce in our office or that email that we are writing can be made more creative.

"Oh really!" I can see your mind going; "Are you serious, Rajen?".

Yes, I am serious about this thought but being serious is not the best way towards creativity! Rather; the best way to be creative is to start loosely connecting with various things to bring about a new perspective. Before we move on to How's of creativity; let's see Why (benefits) of our creative endeavours.

"Everybody born comes from the Creator trailing wisps of glory. We come from the Creator with creativity. I think that each one of us is born with creativity." - Maya Angelou

Benefits of Creativity (or everyday simple creativity)

Even though I haven't as yet experienced all these benefits that I have written here; however it is my firm belief that sooner or later this endeavour of ours will connect us with our roots and will lead us to a better output.

Problem-solving

Once we loosen up and start connecting with various things around us - we can try to take inspiration or ideas from an array of faculties around us. We would be able to observe and apply these ideas quite easily to different problems. E.g. Washing machines being used to make Lassi (sweetened thick buttermilk which is consumed in large parts of India).

Innovation

Innovation is the process that converts an idea or thought into a new product or service which delivers value. Encouraging everyday creativity will create an atmosphere where ideas will take roots and innovation will come about.

"If you look at history, innovation doesn't come just from giving people incentives; it comes from creating environments where their ideas can connect." Steven Johnson

Collaboration

Creativity calls for connecting of ideas and thoughts. More the connection with various ideas and people; more chances of creative ideas producing outputs. Free interactions will lead to better collaboration.

"Creating a better world requires teamwork, partnerships, and collaboration, as we need an entire army of companies to work together to build a better world within the next few decades. This means corporations must embrace the benefits of cooperating with one another." - Simon Mainwaring

Happiness

Creativity is in our roots, We connect with our roots the most; when we are at our creative best. Creativity gives us satisfaction and happiness. Creativity requires us to be open-minded and accept different ideas/views which leads us to a more mature and stable person. When we create, we connect with surroundings and events as well as ourselves - all resulting in we being happier.

"Happiness lies in the joy of achievement and the thrill of creative effort." - Franklin D. Roosevelt

Free from stress

Increased happiness and collaboration, as well as our creative output that is visible, reduce our stress. When we create something we feel the pleasure and fun of it and this reduces stress. We don't feel the pressure of time or commitment nor of stress of competition. We let our creative juices flow freely and in this freedom, we feel burden less and stress-free.

"Don't worry about breaks every 20 minutes ruining your focus on a task. Contrary to what I might have guessed, taking regular breaks from mental tasks actually improves your creativity and productivity. Skipping breaks, on the other hand, leads to stress and fatigue." - Tom Rath

Increased productivity

When we are happy, free from stress and are creating something close to our heart and learning in the process, the definite result is the increased productivity. With innovative and new ways to solve problems; we deliver more things and faster. When we collaborate we achieve the division of happy labour which helps in productivity.

"Creativity Produces Productivity" - Mike Vance

Sense of presence

Creativity gives us perspective of presence where our mind is still. The time seems to be stopping however we don't feel the pressure of time. We get an enhanced impression of this creative time and become calm and feel full presence of ours.

"The state of Presence is the only state in which the creative energy is available to you." - Eckhart Tolle

Self-awareness

Being in present, we get glimpses of our real self - we slowly become aware of our inner self.

Increased morale and Team Bonding

Happy, creative and collaborative atmosphere leads to increased morale and team bonding. Which again intern helps to increased positivity, productivity and happiness. Thus creativity is self-motivating spiral that leads to more positivity, productivity and creativity.

How to go about everyday creativity

Ask Questions and be shameless

Asking questions is the best way to understand new things and ideas. More you ask, more you learn, more you learn, more you can assimilate and synthesize. More you synthesize, more you can let your ideation work and in this process, you begin to feel creative. Don't be afraid to ask - be shameless in learning. It's good for you.

Time Out

Break is the best mind simulator. Continuous working under pressure - saps our energy. We require energy to be creative. So next time you are feeling pressure and lack of energy - take a break. Come back refreshed to the problem - who knows in those 5 minutes you have seen something or met somebody who gives a completely different perspective which helps you to solve the problem at hand with new rigour and creativity.

"Energy is the key to creativity. Energy is the key to life." - William Shatner

Be curious

Curiosity may have killed the cat but believe it will not kill you. Rather it can make you more creative. Curiosity will make you meet new people, see new sights, be an active listener and overall help you in the learning process.

The assimilation of new information and ideas will help you express it more in your outputs.

Diverse information

Unrelated information from your field of work can be good. The serendipity it leads will help you immensely. You will be able to connect various information to problems at hand to solve them creatively.

Travel

Travelling gives us new perspectives, it makes us see different things, see new cultures and meet new people. You will learn about how people go about their lives and what their problems are. We become aware of the world and become more mature. The learning from these sights helps us next time when we see our problems.

Light exercise/walking

Low effort exercise/walking helps us to concentrate and think more effectively and freely. It makes us positive and helps to be more creative.

To do list/pen and paper

Our mind constantly thinks. This can be negative thinking and positive thinking. When it throws out some idea - it would be advisable to catch that, note that down and build upon that.

Everybody gets various ideas - creative people build upon these ideas and others let these ideas go waste.

Meet new people

Meeting the same set of people doesn't give you new information or ideas. You can't be learning new things from the same set of people. Meeting new people will provide you with new information and perspective which is very good for food for thought or creativity.

Stay away from TV

TV is good for entertainment but bad for creativity. Things that we learn from TV is good, but constantly watching TV makes us passive. Surely passivity has never heard to be the birthplace of creativity.

Daydream

Dreaming in day or night is very good. Your mind creates these dreams (thus proving that everybody is a creative person or everyone's mind is already creative!). Daydreaming helps you as you can retain these dreams and utilize the crazy ideas that your brain has provided you.

Listen to music

Music soothes us, relieves stress and makes us calm. In this calmness, our brain becomes active and throws out various ideas. Music being a direct product of creativity also helps us to be more creative. You may have seen artisans such as woodworker or painter listening to music while carrying out their art of labour.

Ignore negativity

Negativity has never been understood to be helping creativity. Creative people by nature are more positive. Thus avoid negativity and negative people.

Understand the perspective

Try to listen to different people and understand them. Only when you understand the different perspective you can apply these in your lives.

Experiment

Finally, creativity is not a milestone but a journey - you can't draw "Mona Lisa" unless you have experimented and failed in this journey. Strive to be creative every moment and experiment a lot. Fail, learn and move on!

What of Creativity?

Hope you are with me so far :-)

We have seen the benefits and process that will help us to be more creative. However, you would say what about Everyday Creativity in our workspace? What about it?

I have a very short answer to that. Let's not deem our existing jobs as jobs where no creativity can be applied. There is nothing in the world which can't be done better, can't be done more creatively. So next time when we are attending a meeting; let's not just make our presence felt by making to the quorum but by asking the right questions. Let's understand the perspective and contribute more.

Let's apply ideas from different streams into our daily life. If you have attended a training in which you have learned storytelling or role play - let's try to apply in our daily life. That email you are about to write - let's read again from the recipient's perspective and try to be more creative and collaborative. Let's not shoot missiles in our emails or reports, but spread ideas and innovation.

Let's be more creative in our daily life.

"Creativity is a habit, and the best creativity is the result of good work habits." - Twyla Tharp

19

EFFICIENCY DRIVERS

"There can be economy only when there is efficiency." - Benjamin Disraeli

Currently, the whole business world is engaged in various efficiency measures and efforts. The innovative technologies, robotics, machine learning methods and various processes improvement philosophies - everybody is engaged in some or other efficiency improvement plan.

All these are kick-started with the right aim in mind i.e. to improve efficiency. However, amid a lot of thrust and activities, the root cause of all these may tend to be forgotten. With various vendors/consultants and technology company selling their wares - it would be advisable to build a proper mechanism to effectively choose these ideas and build on only those which makes sense.

How to go about this? Not very difficult and is very common sense. Here is my collated/suggested drivers.

- **Capacity Creation**: Challenge the idea of how much capacity it would create after it has been implemented. This capacity than can be used for more beneficial activities.
- **Cost Save**: Pure and simple litmus test. What would be the cost savings? (minus the cost of implementation of the idea itself).
- **Cost Avoidance**: Different from cost saving. Here the costs can be altogether avoided - so better than cost saves.

- **Control Enhancement**: Will it improve the controls? Controls are the backbone of any organization - the stronger and effective they are the future costs can be avoided.
- **Risk reduction**: Will our risks reduce? Make day to operations less risky and more predictable?
- **Opening new areas of business/sales opportunity**: if not saving costs then what else? Increasing the top- line. Let's invest only if new sales areas/themes can be identified.
- **Client satisfaction**: No cost saves - no top-line increase? Then surely at least our clients will be happier. If not even these? They why bother!
- **Sales enhancements/cross-selling/value increase**: Finally new business/value delivery principles – the final nail in the coffin - even not achieving this? Then better forget the whole thing.

20

THE "PROBLEM" WITH THE "PROBLEM STATEMENT"

The fact that I have used the word "problem" for referring the subject "problem statement"; itself shows my predicament about the problem statement. That way the problem about the problem statement is very easy i.e. it is problematic. But just making the problem easier doesn't make the problem less problematic.

You get it? Are you with me? Surely you must be wondering "What's happening Rajen?" or rather "What is his problem?"

"You are either part of the solution or part of the problem." - Eldridge Cleaver

Being on the solution side of the problem over the last many years i.e. being a business analyst for many years; I have seen, reviewed, drafted, challenged and delivered on many problem statements. And now through experience and with confidence, I can boldly say that defining the problem statement is not at all easy and most people find it very difficult (or problematic). The most problematic part of the problem statement is that people drafting it completely get it and people reading it generally don't get it. So what are the problems with the problem statement?

Let's review them. Here are the general problems:

It's the "solution"; not the "problem"

We human beings are natural problem solvers; so our tendency jump to the solutions rather than sticking to the problem is quite universal or pervasive. [Did you observe - that I have offered my solution here and haven't explained the problem yet.]

Let's review a classic situation at our home front. Imagine that child comes home after exams and declares that paper was tough and he /she might not fare well in the exam. So what's the immediate reaction from the parents? You know the drill; "I told you so, why you didn't study hard!". What we have seen here - is that we have jumped to solution (or our idea about the solution) instead of understanding the problem, in this example, it would be "appreciating" the problem.

This happens in the office as well. "Sales are down! We need to expand our market reach by adding more salespersons". What is required here? The sales are down with respect to (w.r.t) other company? year? period? and by how much and etc. But when we sit down to define the problem statement - we define the solution!

"I Would Spend 55 Minutes Defining the Problem and then Five Minutes Solving It." - Albert Einstein

"Symptoms" and not the "Impacts"

Problem statement typically ends up defining the symptoms of the problem and not the problem itself. A problem typically has the impact (the most important part of the problem statement) but what we end up describing are the symptoms. Again taking the example of an office situation; "Employee attrition is all-time high, surely our competitors must be paying higher salaries than us!". We leave it at that. Employees leaving is not the problem, but generally symptoms of deeper things happening in the company.

"A problem clearly stated is a problem half solved." - Dorothea Brande

It's classified for the learned

Most problem statements use the help of jargon or "big word"- "concepts". If the problem statement can't be described to a layman than its not the real problem statement. Read the following statement.

"Sales funnel is overheated resulting in non-responsiveness of our delivery value chain".

Most problem statements are reserved for the learned. De-jargoning them will help to define the problem.

Let me try with the above statement.

"We are not able to respond to customers due to volume of inquiries...resulting ....."write your impact".

"The only difference between a problem and a solution is that people understand the solution." - Dorothea Brande

Everything under the "sun"

Problem statement includes everything possible so much so that it loses total relevance. Given the opportunity, we include all the problems in it rather than being specific to the problem area. We want to be safe than sorry. But then that's the problem, if we can't be specific then we can't define a good problem statement. Resulting in poor understanding and bad solutions.

"There is no such thing as a bad solution, but only the bad problems." - Anonymous

21

MAKE A HALF-HEARTED ATTEMPT

Imagine that you have been put into a new situation. A new project, new work, a new challenge or even a new product. People around you are in the same boat. There is little clarity as to how to go about doing the new stuff and what will be the outcome. What happens?

Typically people spend time in meetings and prepare plans to chart out the perfect path. Minutes are kept and hours get lost and the time of 1st deliverables is approaching near. Nothing moves but there is a lot of activity.

Sounds too familiar?

"If you don't know where you're going, any road will take you there." - Cheshire Cat to Alice

So what's the solution?

My suggestion is to take the lead and do something, produce something, prepare something and let it be there in open for people to review/respond/challenge or even ridicule you. This attempt can be half-hearted and not a fully planned one.

Reason? To remove the inertia, to give people something tangible to think and challenge, to put a baseline and make people come out of their zone of non-contribution.

"The way to get started is to quit talking and begin doing." - Walt Disney

This is not easy; not many people attempt. why?

Multiple reasons: (1) fear (2) why me? (3) why bother (4) above my pay grade (5) nobody knows (6) lack of ownership (7) confusion etc.

However, I would suggest to overrule the above reasons and do something.

"You don't learn to walk by following rules. You learn by doing, and by falling over." - Richard Branson

22

ON CREATING PRESENTATIONS

"My best advice is to not start in PowerPoint. Presentation tools force you to think through information linearly, and you really need to start by thinking of the whole instead of the individual lines." - Nancy Duarte

Enough is written on the need and the usage of presentations in all walks of life. Presentation has become as normal as brushing your teeth. If you are in office or in a media industry (or for that matter anywhere else), there is little doubt that you will be creating at least one presentation per week.

In short, we all are already experts in presentations (a.k.a ppts) so then you will wonder what this essay is about? Here I am going to summarize my thoughts on types, methods and ways/means to go about creating presentations.

"PowerPoint may not be of any use for you in a presentation, but it may liberate you in another way, an artistic way. Who knows." - David Byrne

Let's understand the types of presentations. At times I have seen that people do get confused about this matter. I believe the following categorization is also provided in MS PowerPoint - but I will simplify them further.

Always question what kind of presentation is required? Most of the time the presentation that we create in an office setting is a record presentation (i.e. for record-keeping/evidence/ governance-related) but we may end up creating a show presentation which may not go down well with the audience.

Types of presentations:

Show (or sell) presentation

These are created for selling ideas in a meeting room setting / or in video conference. To be used when you are pitching for some idea/concept that you want approval for. Typically these will have max 5 slides on the main concept and supporting 15 slides. You can include animation and clip art/pictures (again depending upon audience). Font is generally quite big 16+.

Message is the key here. What is that you want?

However if this is printed and distributed you may lose your punch - so you may need a supporting read presentation as well. (More below)

Read presentation

Typically these are for offline reading. Many times there is a meeting where these are discussed but there is limited need of actual "presenting" - the meeting may require somebody to take a lead and read out some slides but the expectation is that the meeting audience has already read the content. Not many pictures/clip art expected. Animation definitely "no". These are typically small fonts (10/12) - at times are 8 as well. The length depends upon materials - I have seen 100+ pages as well. Message is not a big focus - but you may want to convince the readers about positive or negative achievements etc.

Update/Teach/Training presentation

These are used for typical training or update kind of setting. Mostly mix of both Show and Read. Will include pictures/clip art/animation as well as some external video links etc. May include part of a read presentation (as pre-read or post-read). Font again will be big 14++.

Message is drafted to achieve the purpose.

Record presentation (evidence presentation)

Again these are read presentations but only read++. These are created for record-keeping/ evidence purposes. In the old days, these would have been created in MS Word. But with presentation tools' usage increasing these "record or report" are also created in presentation mode. Nothing wrong with this. Again these can go quite big with multiple slides/sections/topics. Limited pictures. Small fonts. Message is critically drafted to achieve the main purpose.

> *"If you like overheads, you'll love PowerPoint." - Edward Tufte*

We have understood the types.

Let's see the common issues faced by all of us and how to avoid them.

What's the message?

While we get engrossed in creating a beautiful presentation - at times we forget the critical aspect of the presentation i.e. what is that we want? what you want to convey?

Match the audience

Your presentation should match the taste of your audience. The presentation is not for showing your skills in creating presentations but matching the audience's expectations. e.g. if your audience doesn't prefer many clip arts then definitely that is your takeaway. Don't include clip arts or pictures.

Too Detailed

This is classic and has happened with me many times. Whenever I have created presentations, my bosses have found those to be too detailed. We put all our knowledge into presentations as if somebody is testing our knowledge on the subject matter. We put a lot of charts and figures - which may not be necessary.

Hiding behind details

At times we put a lot of details/figures as if we are hiding behind these. The main message even if known is deliberately hidden. If this is strategic - then maybe it is fine - but if this is because of our hesitation - then not a good idea.

Contradictions within the presentation

Again this has happened with me. On slide 3 we would give a very good picture of the progress to all other evidence presented on slide 7 to 12 showing contrary!

Slide handover / in meeting sequence not agreed

If there are multiple presenters, then the sequence or slide handover should be agreed before the meeting. I have seen that these questions are asked in the meetings :-)

Thinking through presentation

Ideally. our thoughts about presentation should be constructed offline (pen and paper!) and then we should go about creating the presentations. But do we do this? We open the presentation and think through it!

"The most used program in computers and education is PowerPoint. What are you learning about the nature of the medium by knowing how do to a great PowerPoint presentation? Nothing. It certainly doesn't teach you how to think critically about living in a culture of simulation." – Sheery Turkle

23

On Meetings

"Let's spend some more time; surely we can't arrive at the correct decision in only 45 minutes" – Anonymous

Whether you are in a business or working in a factory or the outdoor construction activity; you have to attend meetings to get things done, convey status, follow instructions and share updates/information. We all understand the importance of meetings. But deep there we do have a feeling that these may not that effective, at least not for the full time that they are set in motion. Thus this essay; here I am going to summarise my current thinking on this topic. I have not implemented all the thoughts that I am going to write here - but genuine attempts are being made. Most of these are written from the meeting host's viewpoint i.e. what one should do when one is calling for the meeting.

"We were hoping that you couldn't join the meeting, and we would assign some actions to you" - anonymous

Some basic structuring thoughts

Nothing new, here I am summarizing some organisational stuff that we all already know.

- **Meeting with a purpose**: meetings should have a purpose (there may be a published/well-known purpose and a hidden purpose) - and that purpose should be identified by the host.

Once the meeting is over - the host can do a self-assessment whether the purpose is achieved. If there is pre-reading required then materials can be sent in advance. Also if there is a standing meeting, say weekly, and for one week there is no agenda then it should be cancelled.

- **Meeting with a well-defined venue (digital or face to face)**: Nothing to elaborate on. All participants should know the venue and time in advance. With exception - ad hoc or urgent meeting.
- **Chunks of time**: I assess that most meetings should finish in 25 minutes (at times I wish MS outlook allows setting up meetings for 23 / 27 or 25 minutes slots). Longer meetings should provide sufficient break for people to gather thoughts/ walkabout or go for small breaks.
- **Attendance**: My thumb rule has been 80% attendance is good enough. Many times (and my pet peeve) people don't respond to meeting requests so you are hanging with that unknown whether people will turn up or not. If some members presence is critical then please let them know in advance - and if you don't find them joining then cancel those meetings (or push back to another day).
- **Format of the meeting**: Meetings differ per their agenda and participants. Some meetings are quite formal say with auditor or external parties while some meetings say with your team will be (or should be informal). It would be advisable to decide the format as well as the agenda/minutes structure beforehand.

"Wow, what we have achieved in this meeting is just next to a well-written email." - anonymous

During the Meeting:

- **Sticking to the brief**: Based on the format (i.e. formal/ informal) - the host should ensure that critical stuff is getting discussed within the first 12 minutes. If the host feels that the meeting is not sticking to the agenda the host must bring back to the agenda.

- **Hidden purpose** host would know the hidden purpose (e.g. in a staff meeting - you want to know the motivation level of the team) that needs to be achieved. So a watch on that.
- **Equal rights?:** Unless otherwise specified about the hierarchy of the participants in the meeting - host should make sure that everybody gets (but not should) opportunity to speak (and nobody takes everybody for a ride :-) and share the ideas. After all, the purpose of the meeting is just that.
- **Actions:** If actions are being assigned (true for 95% of the meeting) then note that only one individual is assigned a particular action and that too with a due date. Assignment of action to two or more people will most likely ensure that the action is not completed on time.
- **Time check - 21 minutes and 53 minutes (and so on):** a time-check should be done at 21st minutes (for 25/30 minutes meeting) and so on - to ensure 80% of the agenda is covered. If more time is needed (for 20%) then instead of calling another meeting - just extend by 5/10 minutes or suggest that other items will be taken offline over emails, etc.
- **Scoring of the meeting:** this is something that I am yet to begin. But if you feel that meeting is quite successful then one should congratulate all the participants and thank all members. If some meeting doesn't achieve the purpose - let the participants know.
- **Wrap up:** please keep at least 3/4 minutes for wrapping up. It would be a good practice to spell out the actions that are assigned with due dates.

"No, I don't know what is happening in the organization, I have been moving from a meeting to meeting." – Rajen B. Harani

After the meeting:

- **Minutes**: 5 hours for informal minutes (just bullet list I guess) and 48 hours for the formal ones should be the target for sending out minutes.
- **Calling for agenda items**: if agenda items are to be solicited then should be done immediately after a meeting i.e. well before the next meeting
- **Follow up** on actions before the next meeting: action status should be asked before the next meeting.

24

AND YES, THE MI AND REPORTS

Let me start with the best quote that summarizes my predicament on MI and reports.

"In God we trust. All others must bring data." – W Edwards Deming

Just to narrow the topic or a disclaimer - this essay covers all Management Information and reports that get produced internally within an organization for its internal consumption. I am not covering the reports which are mandated to be delivered regulators or for various legal compliance.

Before I go ahead - let me offer my definition of MI and Reports: "any information collation, representation and report produced in any format (e.g. excel, ppt, manual) that is not directly consumed from its source and requires effort to produce".

So what about these? My contention is that (which is, of course, is based on my 2 decades of experience) we have too many reports which take a lot of efforts without justifying these efforts.

Now let's see what we can do about this.

Encourage usage of single source: this may require members to access the software for which the software was built! E.g. a suppliers report can be easily accessed from the accounting software instead of creating another excel to present this

Define frequency: whenever asked to produce an ad hoc report - ask for frequency of that report. If a report is required frequently - better to get that auto produced from the source.

Spell out efforts / or put efforts required to produce as a filed on the report: this will make the users/requestor to be conscious of the efforts required

Define standard formats of commonly used reports: many times I have seen the formatting efforts take more time than actually getting the data in order. If reporting standards are defined at the organizational level then these efforts will be reduced.

Challenge the purpose: when asked for the report - ask back the purpose. If a similar report already exists then encourage use of that.

Ask inference that user wants to derive: many times a report is demanded but the user doesn't have a concrete idea about the inference he/she wants to draw. Any report without the inference idea - is purposeless.

Discourage reporters: Overtime there are chances that report producer will produce more reports to justify their efforts/value addition - discourage them and move them towards other value-adding activities

"What we have is a data glut." – Vernor Vinge

Let's see the constituents of a report / what a best report should have:

Complete (focuses on inference): A report that captures the essence of the inference and provides complete data

Timely: a report that is timely e.g. you are meeting a client for recovery and you don't have data available - then what is the purpose of that meeting?

As near to the source as possible: just like Chinese whisper data tends to get morphed into something other than the original format as it travels far from its source

Produced once and used many times/many people: a good, complete and timely report can be used many times

Standard format: Ideally in the standard format

"The goal is to turn data into information, and information into insight." – Carly Fiorina

25

HOW TO GIVE AND RECEIVE FEEDBACK

"Feedback is the breakfast of champions." - *Ken Blanchard*

We all receive feedback from the world and likewise provide feedback to the world regularly. Your likes about others, other's likes about you, restaurants asking to rate their service /food or your clients shouting at you for poor workmanship/late delivery or your kid complaining about too much "green" stuff in the food you cooked - all these receiving and giving feedback is constantly going on.

Whether you are employed in a corporate organization or a social media user or a school going student you will receive some sort of feedback. When you are a client you give feedback to your supplier, when you are a teacher you evaluate your students' performance and as a parent, you give feedback to your kids on a nearly everyday basis.

To come to the point - feedback is all-pervasive and constant. Most feedback is well-intended and is directed to get you improving and your feedback is to improve others. However, we don't see that happening often. Most feedback (when it is not completely all thumbs up) is either neglected or even frowned upon. In the end neither the feedback giver is happy (as the feedback is wasted) not the receiver (as he/she feels evaluated and rated sub-standard).

Ever wondered why so?

In my opinion (through the culmination of various readings of books/articles and thinking) the basic fault lies in how the feedback is given or taken.

"I think it's very important to have a feedback loop, where you're constantly thinking about what you've done and how you could be doing it better." - Elon Musk

Let me explain my views (again some sort of feedback :-)

Classify Feedback into:

Skill related Feedback: Focus on the skill that is the question. E.g. Instead of telling your child that "he/she is bad at studies"; turn the feedback into a positive and how he/she can improve the situation by improving "the additional skills to improve the overall scores in mathematics".

When you are receiving feedback try to decipher the feedback into the improvements that you require in your skill development rather than view the feedback as you are an underperformer. E.g. when someone tells you that you are a poor presenter; try to filter out the noise and find what skills; say bring more impact with voice modulation; that you can improve.

Process related Feedback: Focus on the "process" which went wrong in the delivery of services/goods when giving feedback. This way you can directly come to positives (what can be improved) and are not judgmental. Likewise, when receiving feedback in the form generalities; focus on filtering the process related improvements that you can focus.

Behaviour related Feedback: Most likely in office or school setting; try to reason with feedback receiver that apart from such as such behaviour that can become a hindrance in the progress and can be improved; nothing is personally wrong. Improving behaviour is possible and is direct/positive feedback which can be implemented. E.g. when say a typical member of your team always late to deliver his/her part of deliverable; give feedback relating to how to increase the sense of ownership and passion and not general feedback that you are becoming a bottleneck and are a poor performer.

When receiving feedback see what behaviour traits that you can improve and don't take the feedback always on face-value.

Set the Stage:

Try to set the stage or build the occasion to give feedback so that it hits the target rather than just being casual about the feedback. Casual and off the cuff feedback is never taken as serious feedback.

In Private (never in public):

Most improvements related feedback is supposed to be given in private. When given in public they are mostly perceived as humiliation.

Understand the dosage as per the patient:

All human beings are different. You can't administer the same amount or severity of the dosage to everybody. When giving feedback be mindful of the recipient's appetite and bouncing back abilities.

Other Important Points - Written from the giver's point of view:

- *Be Specific*: Simply put don't beat around the bush - just be plain and simple "on the topic"
- *Be Positive/Non-judgmental*: Remember you intend to improve the situation/performance - so don't spoil the atmosphere and create negativity. Be Positive and focus more on "the improvements" rather than "what went wrong"
- *Pat on the back*: Feedback should not just be given when things are going wrong; but also when they are good right. Thus don't turn your feedback into only improvements related but focus also on recognition and awards
- *Be Timely*: Closer to the event or situation; better the chances of rebounding and improving - so time your feedback
- *Be Regular*: Once in a blue moon feedback in office/school setting doesn't add much value and typically is seen as a tick in the box exercise. Regular feedback with constant check on last feedback's response is quite useful.
- *Be Aligned to Goals*: Your feedback and ultimate goals of organization/team has to be aligned else feedback is wasted, and at worse is wrong
- *Do as you preach*: Surely don't get seen doing the things exact opposite what you preach
- *Be Aware (of your mental state)*: Even though timely feedback is necessary but we aware of your mental emotional state before giving feedback. Giving feedback In the heat of the moment is not recommended

Other Important Points - Written from the receiver's point of view:

"Examine what is said and not who speaks." – African proverb

- *Be Attentive (focus on the message and not necessary medium or choice of words)*: When receiving feedback try to be attentive to the message. Don't focus too much on how the feedback is given but focus on "what is being given"

- *Be Aware (of your mental state)*: When receiving feedback try to be emotionally aware of your situation. If you get too much agitated then the feedback will be lost
- *Be in the others shoes' (the litmus test)*: When receiving feedback - try to be in feedback giver's shoes. If you can do this role play in your head and come back with some feedback then definitely the feedback is good for you
- *Be Positive*: The feedback is not the end of the world and you can improve/ bounce back. Try to get specific points that you can act upon
- *Be Silent*: When receiving verbal feedback - the silence is golden. It is generally proven that if your mouth is open then your ears are generally closed

"Criticism may not be agreeable, but it is necessary. It fulfils the same function as pain in the human body. It calls attention to an unhealthy state of things." – Winston Churchill

26

BRINGING THINGS TO CLOSURE

This essay is based on my experiences and especially my experiences of not bringing things to a close e.g. writing this essay on "how to bring things to closure".

Ironical isn't it? :-)

Anyways; they say learning from one's own mistake is the best form of comeback that one can do - so here I am writing an essay on bringing things to closure.

"I love deadlines. I love the whooshing noise they make as they go by." — Douglas Adams,

We all must have experienced (either in our professional or our personal life) that sometimes things just linger; the decisions are not made and effective closure is not in the sight. Many times there may not be any obvious reason for such to happen. Here in this essay, I will be attempting to explain my understanding of such situations and what we can do about these?

So what happens when things are not brought to a close?

- People spend a lot of energy in doing stuff but not necessarily achieve any results
- Lack of direction or sense of purpose
- Preference given to status quo
- Things are in limbo

- Lingering feeling - coming back to a circle
- In the professional world – a lot of meetings, minutes where hours are lost
- Lack of motivation may cause people to search for other activities/organisations
- Mental pressure of something to be done - but frustration of not completing it

"I like work: it fascinates me. I can sit and look at it for hours." — Jerome K. Jerome

Why things go in limbo?

Again there may not be any obvious reasons for things to be in limbo. However, generally you will observe the following situations:

- *Premature start* - things require the right time to start to bring to a close. It's good to be that early bird that catches the worms, but at times these worms may not have hatched yet!
- *No clear decision-maker* - typically when a new group, department or organisation forms - there may not be a clear definition of a decision-maker or authority yet defined. In this situation even though people try their best but due to lack of authority, the things linger.
- *No upside for decision- maker* - again in a situation where there is a general feeling that whatever will be done; things will turn worse than decisions are hard to come by and things go for a stalemate.
- *Status quo - who will bell the cat?* - even when you have a decision or direction but if that is against the status quo it's hugely difficult to challenge this. This may be due to the culture of that organization or department.
- *Joint ownership/committee working* - if things are under collective governance or ownership (committee decision

type) then generally the path of least resistance is taken - which may cause things to be a limbo for long.

- *No open dialogue* - many a time's inter-departmental dialogue or discussions are formal or non-existence - in this case, things work on assumptions and experience. You all must have seen that cartoon strip where two teams building train tracks from opposite direction get it completely wrong!
- *No deadline* - work expands to fill the time available. So typically people see that there is no deadline - they will keep on working (!) without much result.
- *Unknown work/challenge* - nobody wants to start unknown work and fail.

"Don't mistake activity with achievement." — John Wooden

So we are in the soup! what to do?

Without sounding preaching; here what I have started doing (and failing miserably intermittently) in my sphere of things to bring things out of limbo and bring things to closure.

"You have to develop your whole game to completion." - Isaiah Thomas

- Single ownership for each task - joint ownership of a task generally doesn't work.
- Give deadlines and give them liberally - give deadlines and give for each task; don't keep any tasks without a clear deadline.
- Plan the tasks - Gantt chart them - don't start all project tasks at one go - that way the fear of starting a task prematurely will not arise.
- Define where the buck stops (ownership) - make it known that the ownership is with and at so and so person. That way people know who is at the helm.

- Start - fail - but - push on - encourage people who plunge and take start. This works for unknown or new tasks.
- Encourage decision making - don't be a bottleneck - encourage people to take decisions and press on
- Show and Tell - always try to make a spectacle and declare the deadline of the work. You may have seen that some work at your home e.g. painting your house. Unless you declare a date (especially some auspicious pooja or ceremony); the contractors will not take any date seriously. Through your show and tell and serious commitment of that date - you can give a clear message to finish the work by that date!
- Encourage talking, dialogue- let your team members and other team's talk, more they talk and share - more the problems will be known upfront and more things will not stand in limbo.
- Reward and celebrate closure - once a major milestone is achieved; do celebrate. This over time builds a culture of bringing things to a closure and completing the stuff.

"I think I can recognize when a piece is at a state of completion." - Geoff Dyer

27

COMMUNICATION – THE EVER-DIFFICULT CRAFT

"The single biggest problem in communication is the illusion that it has taken place." - George Bernard Shaw

We all must have faced situations where we feel that our message is not getting across, that our communication has failed, that the recipient just doesn't get the message! If you have faced these situations than welcome to the "how to master (or just improve) the craft of communication club".

Communication is very basic to our existence, very core to humanity (even true in the animal kingdom) - yet we find that it is becoming (or was always - don't know - I have been here from last few decades) ever difficult to communicate. We have more gadgets, more facilities and more time at our hand [don't look at me - count your hours on social media - including this one :-)] – still, communication is becoming very difficult.

This essay is going to explore my thoughts and ideas as to how to improve communication. In the school of communication, I am still in the kindergarten but would like to just list down a few ideas that I have built, read and seen in the real world.

"Don't tell me the moon is shining; show me the glint of light on broken glass." - Anton Chekhov

Problems or Barriers to communication

Before we discuss the thoughts around "how to improve" communication - let's explore what are the problems with communication.

Jargon: Easiest way to disengage the recipient is to use too many jargons or Three letter acronyms (TLAs) or technical language.

Unwanted reference: We all love story or background - but if your background has taken away all the attention span then your subsequent message is going to get lost.

Two-way process: Completely missing the point that communication is a two-way process. The encoding and decoding of message exchange is continuous between two people.

Judging the person/missing empathy: If you don't demonstrate empathy through your voice/body language then communication will fail.

Distractions: Too many distractions - more in this world of gadgets/multi-tasking.

Communication vs. Noise: Are we communicating or just creating noise? Not drafting the message right.

Overload: Anyways the world is overloaded with information - why add more?

> *First, learn the meaning of what you say, and then speak - Epictetus*

Just talking/delivering is not communication: Purely talking and delivering your message is not communication - if the recipient has not understood then it is the failure of communication.

How to improve communication - my thoughts

Always go with the end in mind: My 1st suggestion is to draft your message creatively and with the end in mind. Each communicator has a purpose and when we know this then the half the job is done. Classify your communication (in your mind) and then create your message constructively around this "purpose/end".

My current classifications are as follows:

Recipient should act (drive action): If you want the recipient to take action then craft your communication clearly to bring this out. I have seen many messages which are unclear as to who and what needs to be done - which doesn't help anybody. Be clear as to what and when needs to be done by who and why?

Recipient should decide (decision driven): You want the recipient to decide on something but if the ask is not explicit then the communication with fail. Be very specific about the decision and if possible add pros and cons.

Agree or disagree: You want to demonstrate your agreement/disagreement or derive agreement or disagreement then bring these aspects out. You may wish to give reasons or get reasons for these disagreements/agreements.

Inference: You want the recipient to take some inference then give it. If you are showing some charts in your sales meeting then give out those inferences. Don't just show a chart and leave it there.

FYI: Let it be known that the message is for now FYI for them. Typically you would like to do this with your bosses to just let them know everything is fine and they don't have to yet come into the play.

Choose your battleground (medium): We all have read or heard that words (i.e. email or text messages) bring out only 7% of the impact, tonality (i.e. telephonic/voice messages) bring out only 38% of the impact and body language (i.e. face to face/Video) bring out 55% of the impact in communication. Yet we may always fall back on safe and secure ground of email/text communication. Meeting people in person is still the best way to communicate ideas/thoughts. Choose your communication battleground wisely!

Timing: This can be read in terms of time during the day or month or year. The point is that for the communication to be effective it has to be delivered on time. Research has suggested that if you want somebody to make a courageous decision then always target when the stomach has a full quota of sugar available. Don't target messaging just before lunch or late in the afternoon before dinner :-)

Scope: Don't cover everything under the sun; inversely don't be so loose that the scope of your communication is vague. If you can't be specific in your communication - who will?

Background: Sometimes needed and sometimes not. The problem with the background or story is that it takes away the little available attention span with the recipient from the message. If you have a punch line then bring it fast else your story will fall flat and the messages will be completely lost.

Level: Courses for the horses. Select the course suiting the horse. When dealing with seniors; bring the message to their level of understanding - come to the high-level facts, establish the scope and give the message directly. When dealing with kids; excite them with message laced with stories.

Subject Matter/Language usage: If specific subject language is usage desired then go for it else make the message easily understandable to a layman. My recent example: I went to buy an air conditioner for my home. The salesman just went into technicality of inverter air-conditioner on some variable speed etc. However only when I asked - so what? He started explaining the real benefit.

What's in for me?: Remember the recipient always has his or her benefit at the heart. If your message has one then bring that out! E.g. you want your boss to decide something - then give the advantages of that to him/her so that decision making is easier. Not all messages will have this available - but try to think from other's points of view and bring this out.

Communicate less - demonstrate more: If possible try to avoid the communication and directly provide the demo / final product. The classical dialogue from western movie - "When you want to shoot - shoot. Don't talk!".

Use informal channels: Don't make everything very official. Use your informal channels. These channels provide richer information exchange platforms.

"Science may never come up with a better office communication system than the coffee break." - Earl Wilson

There may be more ideas. My journey to improve my communication is on-going and I am hopeful that I will overcome my shortcomings and improve.

28

DELEGATION
THE DIFFICULT DUTY

"The inability to delegate is one of the biggest problems I see with managers at all levels" - Eli Broad

Like Eli says in this quote, and I also feel that delegation is one of the toughest management traits that are out there. The notion that someone else is equally (or even better!) capable of the tasks that you can do is horrid!

We all love to do things ourselves as it ensures control (and quality/timeliness). We all do this - but then when you have members in your team (whom you may have hired!) who are capable to carry out the burden as well clear your time so that you can focus on something else; is a very powerful tool. But then at the same time, it is also very difficult.

Thus this essay - here in this small essay I am going to describe my ideas (some read and some thought) about delegation and how we all can go about it.

"When in doubt, mumble; when in trouble, delegate; when in charge, ponder." - James Boren

First, let's see what delegation is not.

- delegation is not the same as work distribution or task assignment
- delegation is not remote management

- delegation is not finding a scapegoat just in case things go wrong :-(

So what is delegation?

- delegation is of the outcome (~ne the tasks) - one can't delegate a part of the stuff - it has to be end to end along with outcome (positive or negative)
- delegation is always supported by authority and responsibly (else it becomes task allocation)
- delegation goes along with risks (how true!)
- delegation may be time-specific or work package-specific (but again with authority)

"I don't have a problem with delegation. I love to delegate. I am either lazy enough, or busy enough, or trusting enough, or congenial enough, that the notion of leaving tasks in someone else's lap doesn't just sound wise to me, it sounds attractive." - John Ortberg

Why delegation? Just in case there are doubts.

- grooming 2nd layer/generation
- free up time for focusing on other stuff
- time crunch for key members
- building team
- retirement/handover planning

Finally how to go about with delegation

- delegate the scenario and outcome
- delegate to willing and right person
- delegate with resources, authority and responsibility

29

DATA: COLLATION, ANALYSIS AND INFERENCE

Thousands of articles in various websites/newspapers, numerous new jobs profiles that are getting created & getting popularized such as data scientists, chief data officer etc. and hundreds of events having data as central theme; illuminate me that we are indeed in the golden era of data. The computing power has now reached its peak such that the data science, machine learning and other data related discipline can carry out some serious stuff.

"We're entering a new world in which data may be more important than software." - Tim O'Reilly

I am as excited as everybody on this front; however, my problem is very fundamental or basic; depending upon where you think from. Fundamental because having data is only the beginning & going onto carry out analysis and inferring something useful or actionable is very core to this data journey; which yet is not fully ironed out and basic because it should be already existing with or without the new science in data journey.

So here I will define the problem statement that I face regularly.

Problem statement (according to me): We all have data (or somehow manage to collate it - albeit quite late in the game) but our inference of this data which should give us some concrete actionable(s) is poor or at times not existing.

"Data is not information, information is not knowledge, knowledge is not understanding, understanding is not wisdom." - Clifford Stoll

Having understood the problem [by now you would have decided whether you agree with me and will continue reading this further or not :-)] let me now describe the reasons which are applicable for most of us for not having inference or having poor inference.

- **Barely managing to get data in order and in time**: I have seen that at times (mostly all times) we are running against time to collate and present data. That month end SLA report, that monthly profit statement, that monthly governance pack - all take effort and time and rework and rework and rework such that we are barely on time. 90% of the time or more goes into collation and presentation of data - leaving very little or no time (and energy) to analyse and infer something out of this.

"To write it, it took three months; to conceive it three minutes; to collect the data in it all my life." - F. Scott Fitzgerald

- **What to infer is position and power-related**: Even if you manage to get data on time; the inference is politically risky and people don't want to willingly engage in this. I will explain this by an example. Suppose you have rolled out a new service whereby you have on-boarded various departments who can now report their issues in your software. You are also responsible for solving these issues on time but hard SLAs are not yet defined. So how you infer an issues line graph which is showing an upward slope? If want to show that all departments have been on-boarded then an upward slope is good. This demonstrates that more and more departments are using this software. If you want to show your resolution time - then your upward slope is not good. Who decides this?

- **Inference is mentally taxing:** Inference takes time, inference takes mental/ thinking power, inference takes decision-making skills. Inference is not easy - requires deep analysis and thinking. Having just spent a lot of time and energy just to collate data and present it - we are not ready to fully engage in this.
- **Inference is not taught/people are not trained:** We all are trained in presentation and data collation. The fancy charts and pivots but haven't been trained or taught domain-specific inference of data.
- **Inference is beyond domain knowledge 101:** drawing inference data specific to domain requires deep knowledge of the subject matter. Assumes that you already are the guru of your subject matter. Similar to a doctor who examines a patient with a throat infection, which can have numerous root causes, the data analyser requires expert domain knowledge. Not everyone is one ... yet.

"Data is the new oil." - Kevin Plank

So now what to do? I am not sure. But here are some pointers which can help us.

- Let's spend less time in collating data and more on analysis/inference
- Let's train ourselves more on analysis
- Let's agree common inferences of data without too much of politics
- Let's not get too involved in presentation that we forget what that presentation was for in the first place
- Let's build domain expertise
- Let's discuss less about data but infer more from data

30

HIRING – SOME BASIC RULES

"Hiring people is like making friends. Pick good ones, and they'll enrich your life. Make bad choices, and they'll bring you down." - Jason Fried

By now I must have reviewed a few thousand CVs, interviewed nearly a thousand candidates and hired at least a few hundred people. And I still believe hiring is not easy and can never be made easy :-)

Some challenges that we all have faced; How do you assess whether a person is the right fit for the job? What are his/her reasons for looking at this particular role? Will the candidate match the tempo of the team? Are we hiring the right candidate? All these and more such questions are repeated in my mind at each interview.

However with several years of experience – I have framed a few rules for myself. These basic rules help me to ensure that every candidate is given due justice, the job description is well understood; the process is smooth and also caters to other challenges that we have seen above.

"When I'm hiring someone I look for magic and a spark. Little things that intuitively give me a gut feeling that this person will go to the ends of the earth to accomplish the task at hand." - Tommy Mottola

Rule # 1: Candidate's CV doesn't tell the "full" story about that candidate to you and Job Description doesn't tell the "full" story about the job to the candidate

- Meeting candidate is unavoidable
- Meeting many candidates for a role is unavoidable
- When a CV is borderline – call that candidate in
- Explain the CV filtering group – what is expected and also what is borderline that is accepted
- Like in sales – the size of funnel will increase the chances of a hit – don't be too rigid with CV filtering

Rule # 2: Don't hire over telephone

- Always meet the candidate face to face - you are hiring a member of your team and not ordering electronic goods
- Body language will tell a lot of stories

Rule # 3: Don't hire in the 1st meeting (unless this is campus kind of recruitment)

- Take time to let the job "sync in" for the candidate (let him/her think over at least 1 or 2 days)
- Take time to think over the candidate's candidature for you (you should think over this at least 1 or 2 days)

Rule # 4: Always make candidate meet at least two people from your hiring team

- This will avoid similarity bias
- Make sure these two people are somewhat different in their thinking – so you get two opinions for the same candidate

Rule # 5: Don't hire just because candidate can join ASAP

- You are hiring a member of your team – take time – “Can join ASAP” can never be your criteria

Rule # 6: Don’t think that candidate need to be plug-n-play on day 1 – Remember that training the candidate post-hiring is your job – Don’t look for 100% perfect match, there isn’t any

- Hiring a candidate will lead to an activity at your end that is called “training” – don’t avoid this
- 100% match is too costly for your process (you will be waiting for a long time for that perfect candidate)

Rule # 7: Go for Passion first, Smartness second and Track record third

- My order (post technical/functional match)
    - Passion
    - Smartness
    - Track record/having done “same” job in the past

Rule # 8: If you are the final decision maker then always explain your hiring team what you are looking for in that role

- Remember rule # 1- Job Description doesn’t tell the “full” story
- Explain your team what are the expectations of the job and the candidate

Rule # 9: If you are not the final decision maker and candidate will work for you then always explain the final decision maker what you are looking for in that role

- You will be responsible for that candidate’s performance so better tell what you need

Rule # 10: Always take your time to explain the role to the candidate and make sure he/she has understood it (by asking the candidate to explain the role back to you)

- Remember rule # 1- Job Description doesn't tell the "full" story
- Candidate need to give you comfort feeling that he/she has understood the role else will lead to expectation mismatch/wrong hiring

Rule # 11: Explain all job-related demands to the candidate

- This is more of a hygiene factor but good for avoiding future problems. Inform candidates about known demands of the job such as; support hours (for any different geographies support), travelling need etc.

Rule # 12: Let the candidate speak the most (I know this is the most difficult)

- I have experienced that many times in the interviewing process, the interviewer ends up talking more than the candidate. This is quite contrary to what should normally happen. Be conscious of this factor.

Rule # 13: Ask real-life examples from candidate about achievements and don't just discuss at philosophy level

- Ask for specifics, go for details and ask corroborative stories of candidates "so-called" wins

Rule # 14: Finally remember

- Hiring is a process where there are no short cuts
- Hiring is judgmental

- Hiring can go wrong

"Time spent on hiring is time well spent." - Robert Half

31

HIRING - SOME ADVANCED RULES

"Although most executives pay lip service to the idea of hiring for cultural fit, few have the courage or discipline to make it the primary criteria for bringing someone into the company." - Patrick Lencioni

I hope to uncover some rules over and about Basic Rules i.e. Advanced rules to be followed while hiring. Also, it was easier to break the hiring rules into two essays ☺

Rule # 1: Don't Hire "You"

Don't try to find your qualities in the candidate. You don't want candidates with the same skill and temperament in your team. When "One" is enough you don't what "Two" of you.

Don't also compare your career journey with the candidate's career journey and make the judgment that he/she has got it on a platter and you had to struggle to get it. This information is of no use while hiring.

Rule # 2: Don't try to undermine the candidate

Don't try to prove that the candidate doesn't know much or can't do much. Try to find out what candidate knows and what he/she can do. Make the interview a positive process.

Your questioning and body language during the interview are as much as important as of the candidate's. You are not just hiring for you alone – there is an organization behind you.

Rule # 3: Don't get easily impressed

Opposite of Rule # 2. Don't just see the confidence, body language and selling ability of the candidate and make the hiring decision. Don't just judge good communication skills and "presence" during the interview but ask questions leading to the core "doing" skills for which you are hiring. Don't let the candidate influence you.

Best way is to ask detailed questions about situations faced in the past and some referrals. If the candidate is making the story then deep dive into any story for 5/10 minutes will unravel the true story. Cross with referrals as well.

Rule # 4: Culture fitment is very important

Always mentally gauge the candidate against the existing culture of the team/organization. This is important and will make or break the team in future. Many times we have seen a single person can be very destructive when it comes to spoiling culture.

As against this – if you want to shake up the culture with this "One" hire then go for it. It is your conscious choice.

Rule # 5: Salary benchmarks need to be maintained

We all know the candidate's (and all your existing members') salary details are confidential. However, this doesn't mean you can hire a single individual breaking all the salary benchmarks. Performance payment is different and same role's salary benchmark is a different concept.

While hiring makes sure that the salary that you offer for a role/grade is at par for that role across your team.

This doesn't stop you to pay out a better bonus to high performing candidate based on his/her performance.

Rule # 6: Encourage referrals

Referral hire (along with giving out referral bonus) is a good concept. It increases loyalty/stickiness to the organization, members feel empowered as their friends/families do talk about their "this" achievement and readily creates well-bonded teams.

However, don't let a single individual/group hogging on referral positions. This will increase "group-ism" in your team.

Rule # 7: Explain the job and way you have thought about it to be done

Especially for a role which is new for your organization. Explain in detail as to what is expected of the role and what style you need to see getting portrayed. More so for middle-tier and senior-level roles.

Explain all the decisions that this role is empowered to take and role's performance criteria. If the role is having fiduciary/legal responsibilities then explain that.

Rule # 8: Once the decision is made – try getting your key people meet candidate - the "new yet to join incumbent"

Let your team know that you have made a key hire decision and make them meet the person. This will build a rapport, clear the air before the person joins and create a ground for the new member.

This will also allow you to sort things out internally well before the new member joins the organization. If this role is senior and/or the client-facing – I would advise letting the candidate meet other senior people / key clients.

"When I meet successful people I ask 100 questions as to what they attribute their success to. It is usually the same: persistence, hard work and hiring good people." - Kiana Tom

32

SOME INTERVIEWING GUIDELINES

"I sometimes find that in interviews you learn more about yourself than the person learned about you." - William Shatner

Surely everybody would know the basic purpose of interviewing any candidate - to assess whether the candidate is fit for the job. However, I would like to add few points onto this line of thought.

Purposes of the interview:

The obvious ones:

1. To assess whether the candidate is fit for the job
2. To figure out current and past behaviours as clues of the future behaviours
3. To find the best suitable candidate amongst many

Not so obvious ones:

1. Not to show off your knowledge, power or stature in the organization or bigness etc. that of the organization to the candidate
   [Believe me, I have seen this happening a lot]
2. Not to test knowledge of the candidate
   [Some knowledge testing is desired - but don't make the full exam out of the interview]

3. Not to know what is happening in the outside world through the interviews
   [Especially the candidates from competitors]

So far so good? Once understood the purpose of the interview we now move towards the guidelines of the interviews.

Guidelines for Interviewing:

Preparation

- Explain HR about the job and the skills that you require. Your brief to them is key to get correct resumes of the candidates.
- Read the Resume of the candidate and make your notes/questions for the candidate.
- Assign time for each interview and stick to that. Also, decide how many rounds of interview will be conducted and who and how the candidate will be decided.
- Prepare other interviewers by explaining to them about the job and skills desired in the candidate. Especially true if many interviews are done in parallel or through panel format.
- Maintain the Momentum of the interviewing process. Don't keep weeks or months between two interviews of the same candidate.

During the interview

- Set the scene - company profile, team, role and expectations
- 70/30 - Remember - let the candidate do the talking (roughly 70% of the time)
- Ask questions:
    - Open-ended
    - Not multiple choice type

    - Purposeful
    - Not leading
    - Appropriate
    - Not abusive/threatening
    - Job-related
    - Such that will help in decision making
- Create a good impression with the candidate - establish rapport
- Try probing into 1 or 2 stories from the past - remember past behaviour generally is a good yardstick for the future
- Ask for candidate's contribution and don't accept answers in generality e.g. "We achieved this"
- Make notes
- Give time to the candidate to ask question and provide truthful answers
- Don't show you have either made up your mind about the candidate or you are indifferent
- Avoid interruptions - definitely don't look at watch/mobile/wall/take a phone call during interview etc.

Close and Selection

- Explain next steps to the candidate
- Discuss with other interviewers and compare their notes - most likely a consensus candidate will emerge else go with the decision maker's choice
- Explain HR the criteria of the selection
- Keep in touch with the selected candidate till the time he/she joins the organization

"Interviewer: Please tell us why you would love to work for us."
"Candidate: I need the money."

ALSO CHECK OUT

NINE LIVES. THREE STORIES. ONE BOOK.
'A book with zero negative reviews till date!'
ONCE
UPON
a
TIME
'A brutally honest saga of love, dreams and real life.'
SAURAV
CHHAWCHHARIA

#ZeroNegativeReviews

"A perfect blend of romance, fiction and thrill. The plot twists and cliffhangers will make sure you finish the book in one sitting. I just can't keep away from it. This is a book you should read if you're a reader and definitely read if you're a writer."

– *Dhwani Parmar*

"The way the life of Samir, Rashid and slums is depicted. And that sweet love story which death overtook even before it started: clearly signifies how your potential can be wasted unknowingly, on the other hand how someone low can emerge out! Man, I want a sequel to this!"

– *Kushal Raut*

"As John Green said and here I quote: *Sometimes, you read a book and it fills you with this weird evangelical zeal, and you become convinced that the shattered world will never be put together unless and until all living humans read the book!* Once Upon A Time is that book. And though I want to smite you for breaking my heart again and again, I can't help but say that I'm thankful that you wrote this and you did a pretty good job in ripping my heart out but thanks anyway!"

– *Anjali Dedha*

To order *– instamojo.com/paperpalace/ouat*